Drawing People

In Zen Doodle Technique

Unleash Your Creativity with Unique Zen Doodle People Drawing

By Daniele Ling

Table of Contents

Disclaimer

While all attempts have been made to verify the information provided in this book, the author does assume any responsibility for errors, omissions, or contrary interpretations of the subject matter contained within. The information provided in this book is for educational and entertainment purposes only. The reader is responsible for his or her own actions and the author does not accept any responsibilities for any liabilities or damages, real or perceived, resulting from the use of this information.

The trademarks that are used are without any consent, and the publication of the trademark is without permission or backing by the trademark owner. All trademarks and brands within this book are for clarifying purposes only and are the owned by the owners themselves, not affiliated with this document.

Introduction

If you have already read about Zen Doodle drawings, this concept of drawing Zen Doodle people would not be new for you. However, if you are new to Zen Doodle, you do not need to worry at all. **Drawing People in Zen Doodle Technique - Unleash Your Creativity with Unique Zen Doodle People Drawing** has been written in such a manner that even if you have lifted the pencil for the first in your life for drawing, you will not face any difficulty in learning.

First thing first, Zen Doodle is not just about filling up a 4"X4" box with random designs. You need to think strategically before you proceed to draw. This does not mean that Zen Doodle is very complicated. It is actually very simple once you get the hang of it. For drawing human figures in this genre, you do not need to learn drawing the details of human features. However, at the least, you must know how to draw human figures in silhouettes.

You might have seen your shadow when you have a bright light at your back. Try drawing your body structure with the reference of that shadow once. You just need to have perfection in drawing only such outlines of people. The remaining drawing can be filled up by extremely easy Zen Doodle designs.

Learning Zen Doodle designs is not difficult at all. You must have scribbled many things on the back page of your notebook in school. That was the beginning of your drawing career. Now, you need to refine those very patterns and incorporate them into your drawings. Sometimes, you might love to think about placing a particular design in a specific location according to the characteristics of that particular location. That would be the time when you would actually learn Zen Doodle.

Now, shed all the temptation to rest, grab your tools and sit down to draw. You will fall in love with Zen Doodle!

Section 1
Chapter 1 - Drawing People

You might have got Goosebumps at the thought of drawing a human figure. It happens with almost every amateur artist on Earth. Even if they are proficient at their work, drawing human figures and especially portrait, makes them nervous before they start. It happens because they are not sure if they can make the sketch look like their subject. This characteristic of "likeliness" seems somewhat hard to achieve. However, in the same scenario drawing a generic human face which does not resemble anyone is a cakewalk for even a kid.

The fear for achieving likeliness roots back to the tendency of our "logical' mind to create symbols. We tend to achieve "perfection" in every human figure we see. Even if our subject has a little imperfection in their nose, we try to convince our mind that the nose does not look like what we are seeing. That is where we commit mistakes. We must trust our eyes and draw what we see, not what we think.

Tips to draw people

Make use of the tips mentioned below to draw people. You will definitely find yourself more at ease.

Drawing hands

You must not forget that there are muscles and bones beneath the skin of hands or any other body part of human body whatsoever. In some parts of the hands, the surface or the skin is affected by the sharp bones and in other parts, by soft muscles. You do not have to round off all the shapes or your subject would look rubbery.

Drawing people or anything else

Drawing grids can never go out of fashion. It is a classic method of drawing exact human figures. It gives you correct proportions of everything you see. You just need to draw a grid on your reference photo and then draw one more grid on your drawing sheet. It gets really painful to erase the grids. Thus, you can also make use of a light box in place of grids. Draw a grid on a plane paper and tape it on the light box. Now you can place your drawing sheet over the light box and conveniently draw whatever you want.

Drawing people

While drawing people, using a midline or a shaft comes in handy. When you draw a midline through a human figure, it gives you an idea of the way it is getting a support. The midline or the shaft behaves like a framework underneath direction and movement. You will also find it simpler to see or indicate the viewpoint of certain forms.

Opposites attract

This is a major principle of design but it also validates itself in the drawings of human figures. Opposites attract means that the symmetrical designs are not so attractive but asymmetrical designs are. You might have noticed in the pictures that if a person is standing with their one shoulder jerked up a little, it looks more interesting than they are simply standing with their both shoulders lying symmetrically in a regular manner. Also, if we lay our weight on one leg, our photographs come out more interesting than they would if we stand with our weight equally poised on both legs. Each opposite assists to clarify and strengthen the other.

How to draw someone?

The muscles form the substructure of our body. They play a major role in how we look and give us form and shape. You need to understand the structure of muscles to understand how you should make the human body and face. You will be able to notice important details which you may not even bother otherwise.

Drawing characters

If you are a visual artist, you need to choose the manner in which you would depict an event- which portions need to be emphasized, which portions need to be downplayed- can be achieved through staging. If you have got sufficient clues like costumes, props or setting; to let you know the interaction of peoples' body language; the onlookers would understand the meaning and story behind your sketches.

Utilize your time efficiently

Do not spend your time studying and drawing unnecessary details; rather spend time studying those details with a keen eye that a layman's eye would not notice. Such intricate details would make your drawing stand out of the rest. For instance, sometimes the background takes a more important place in a drawing than the main subject itself. Similarly, you might find a small scar over the eyebrow of your subject. If you miss it, you will end up making a regular drawing that would not speak for itself. However, if you make use of direction of light and depict that just one scar properly, your sketch would come out alive.

Drawing people in doodle art

The above facts are true for drawing real human figures. In Zen Doodle drawings, you do not have to achieve that perfection or likeliness of human features. Thus, even if you have just laid your hands on pencil and paper, you can still achieve perfection in drawing people in the genre of doodle art. In the further chapters of section 2, you will see that there are some human figures, whose shadows need to be drawn in silhouette. The remaining figures are covered with Zen Doodle designs.

The patterns of Zen Doodle are very simple to draw. You can pick up any design you want and modify it as you like. There are several patterns which are a combination of two or more patterns. When you become proficient at Zen Doodle drawings, you will be able to discover your own designs and incorporate them in your drawings.

Section 2
Chapter 1 - Dancing heart

You might have seen this heart pose of dancers elegantly stretching out their bodies to make a heart shape using the negative area of their pose. While drawing human figures in Zen Doodle, it is true that you do not have to draw any intricate details of faces, or any other parts of the body. But, it is equally true that you cannot ignore the silhouette and the outer shape of the body and face.

Maintaining accuracy in the outline is the key to draw perfect Zen Doodle human figures. The designs that have to be filled in are equally important. They have to be drawn precisely. Otherwise, you will notice that if the designs are not given their due importance, the end results are not very impressive.

Let us start with our first Zen Doodle drawing:

Step 1:
Draw the outline of a couple making a heart shape with their dancing pose. Notice that they are not holding hands as of now. But, the toes of their feet are almost touching each other.

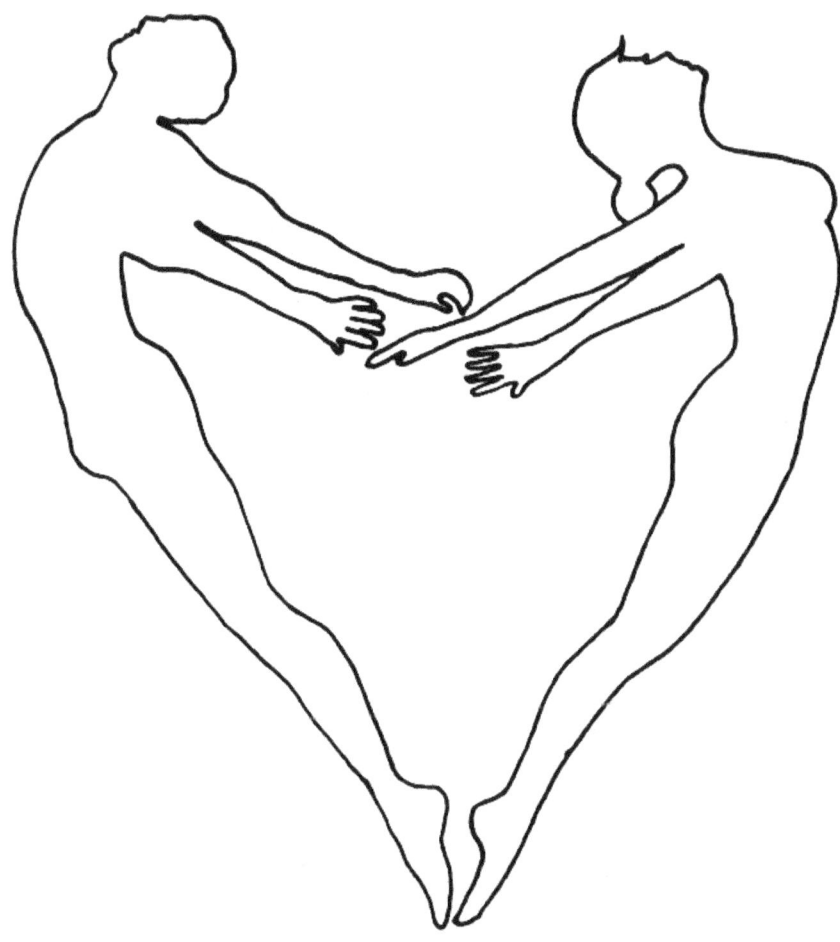

Step 2

In the upper half body of the male figure, draw spirals, ovals with a dot in the center, and some leafy patterns as shown in the figure. Draw some checks in the arm facing you. Cover the hands too with the checks.

In Zen Doodle figures of people, we would not draw realistic features of the body. Instead, we would fill all the body parts with abstract designs.

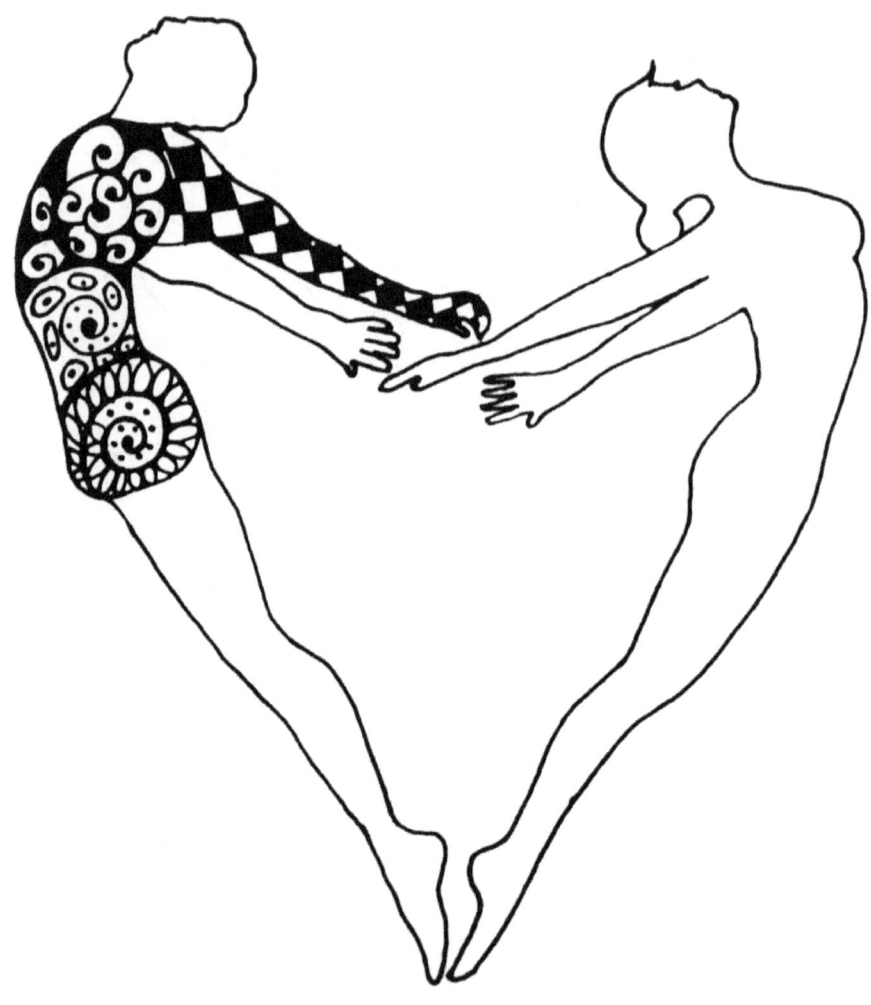

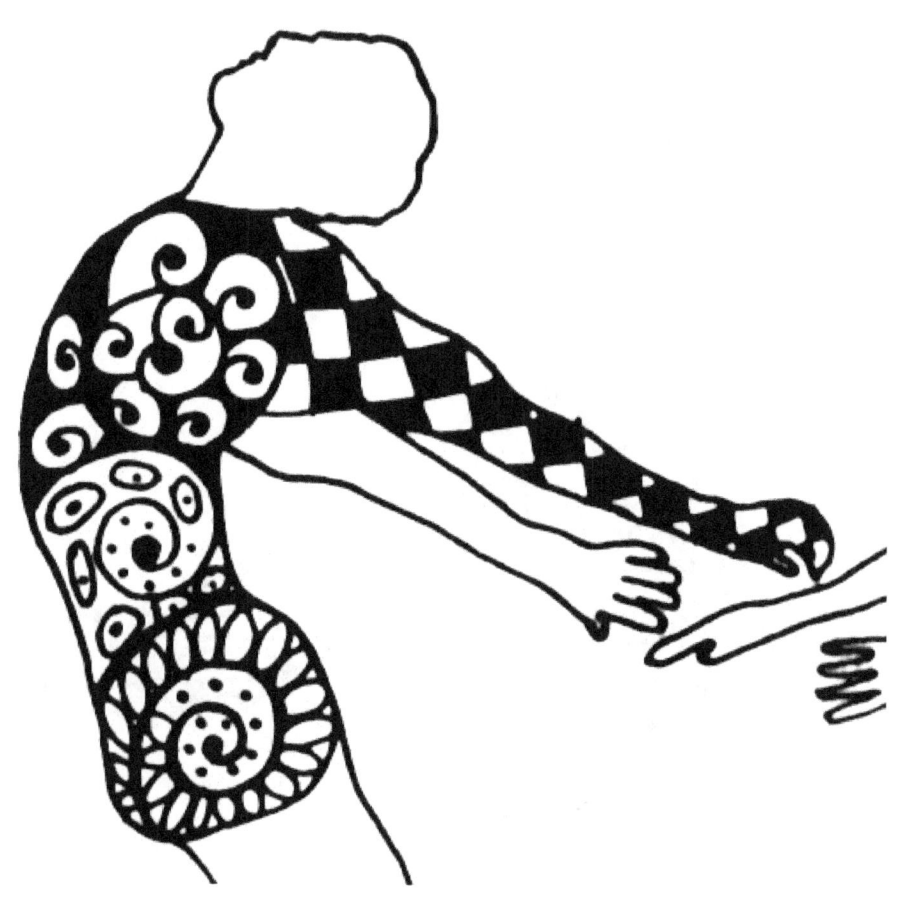

Step 3

In the legs of the male, draw some a stem of graduating leaves and fill them with ink alternatively. Notice that the leaves are getting smaller as they reach the calves and end at the ankles.

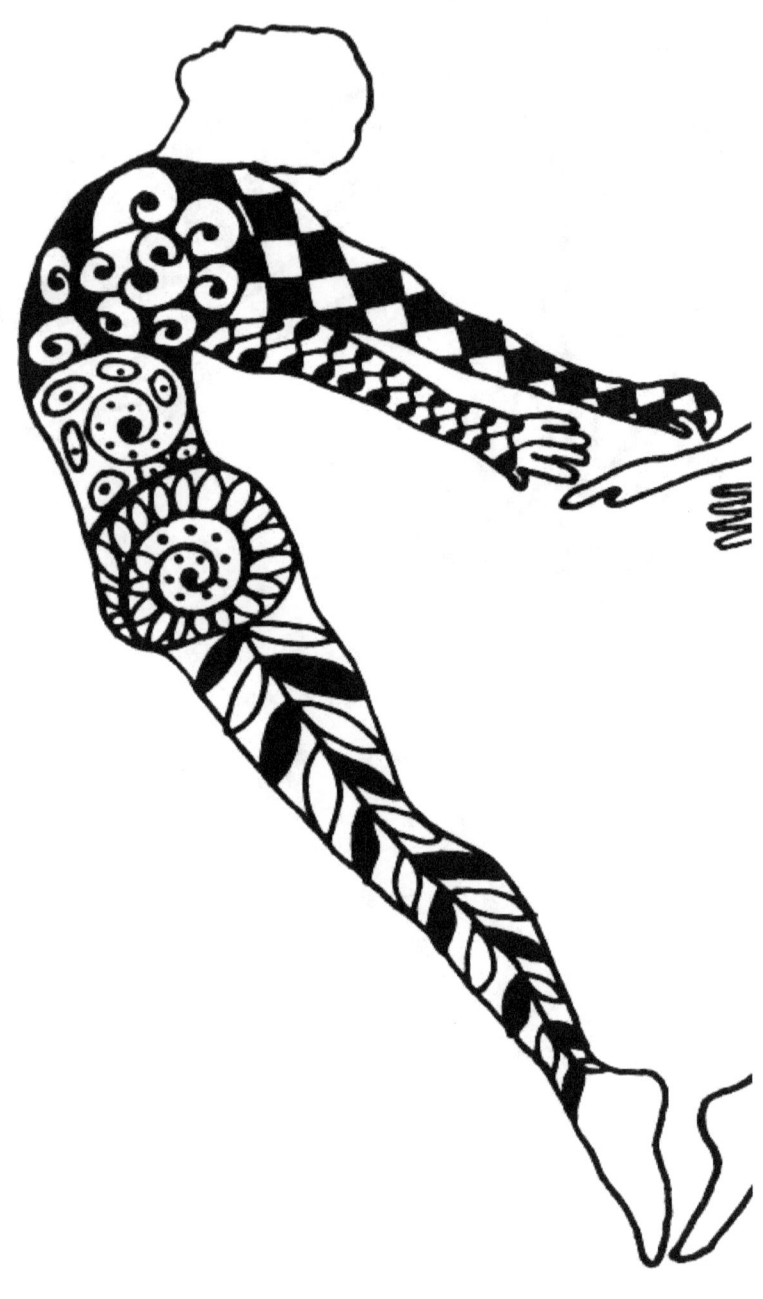

Step 4

Draw a circle and a triangle with bent lines in the foot of the male. Draw a circle in the breast area of the female and draw some leaves around the circle like we do while drawing flowers. Draw bold outlines outside the leaves.

Sometimes, we draw such designs in a particular area of the body which symbolically depict the characteristics of those areas. For instance, we have drawn a partial flower in the breast area because the breasts of a woman are delicate like a flower.

If you can think of any such designs which can be tactfully incorporated in human figures, nothing is better than that.

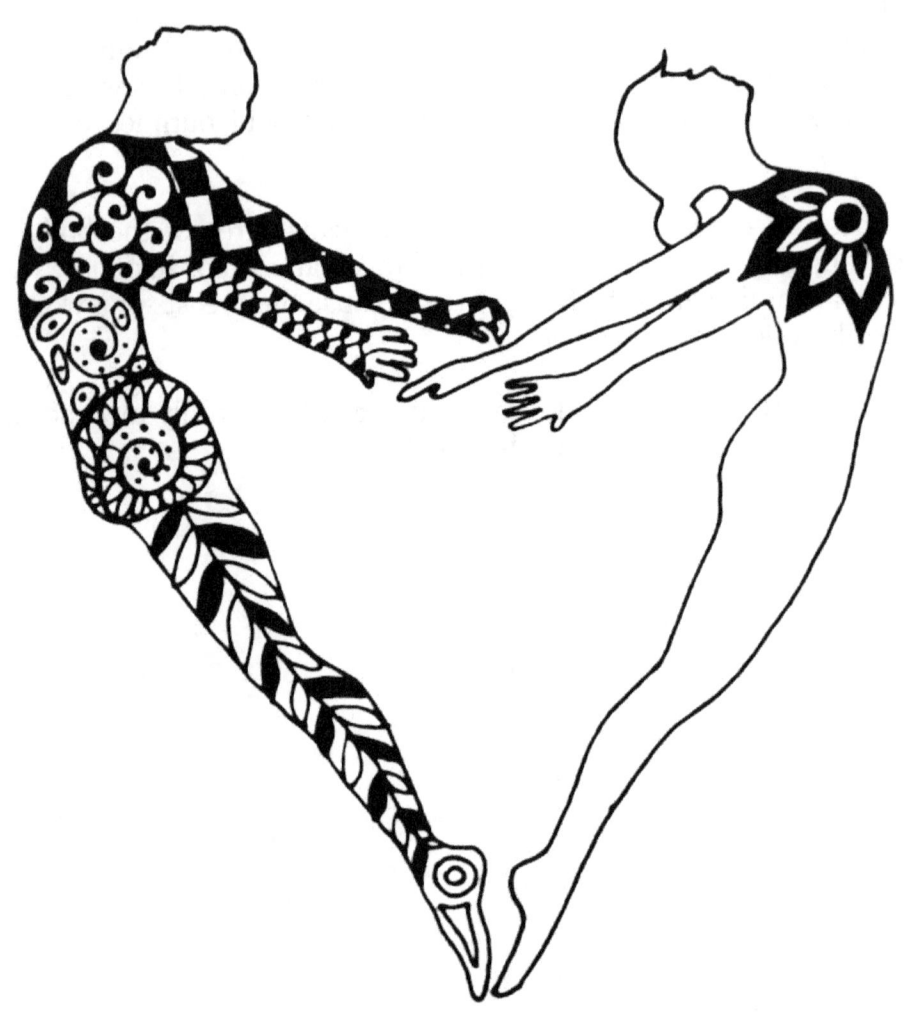

Step 5

Draw a small leaf without the leaf stalk or petiole in the waist portion of the female and fill it up with ink. Taking this small leaf as a base, draw concentric leaves and fill them up with different designs like dots, zigzag patterns, and lines.

Let the leaf stretch almost till the flower in the breast portion and end almost near the knee.

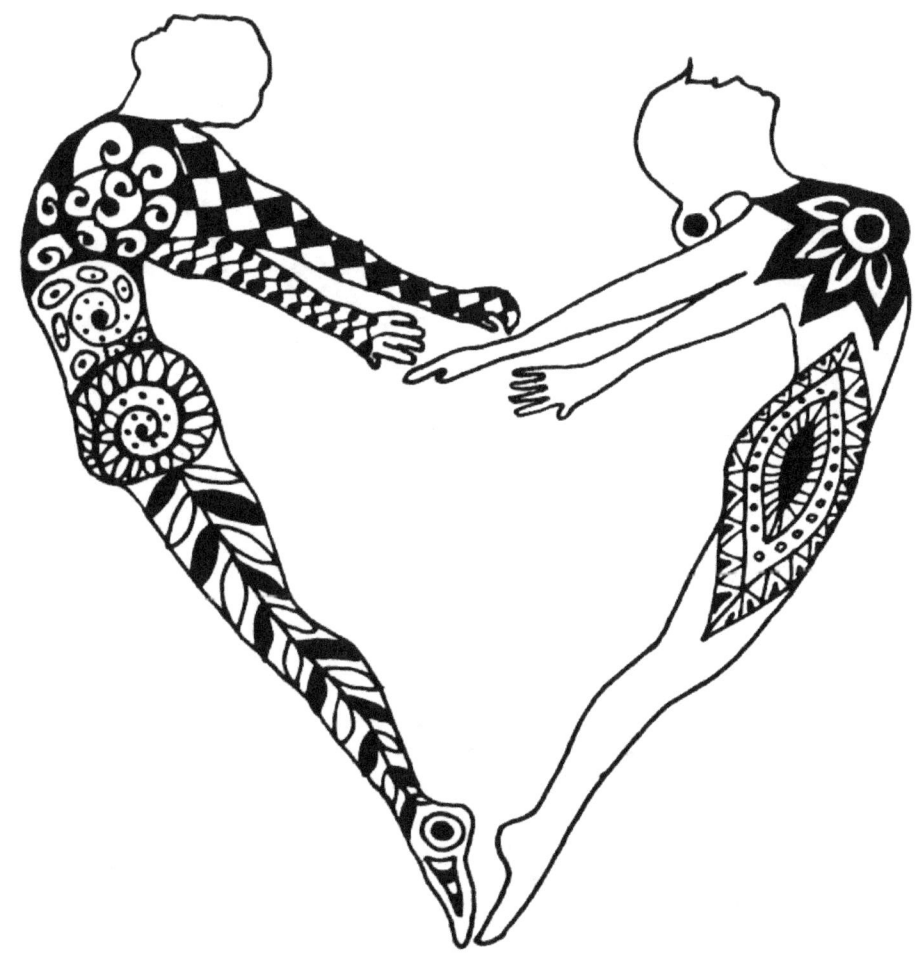

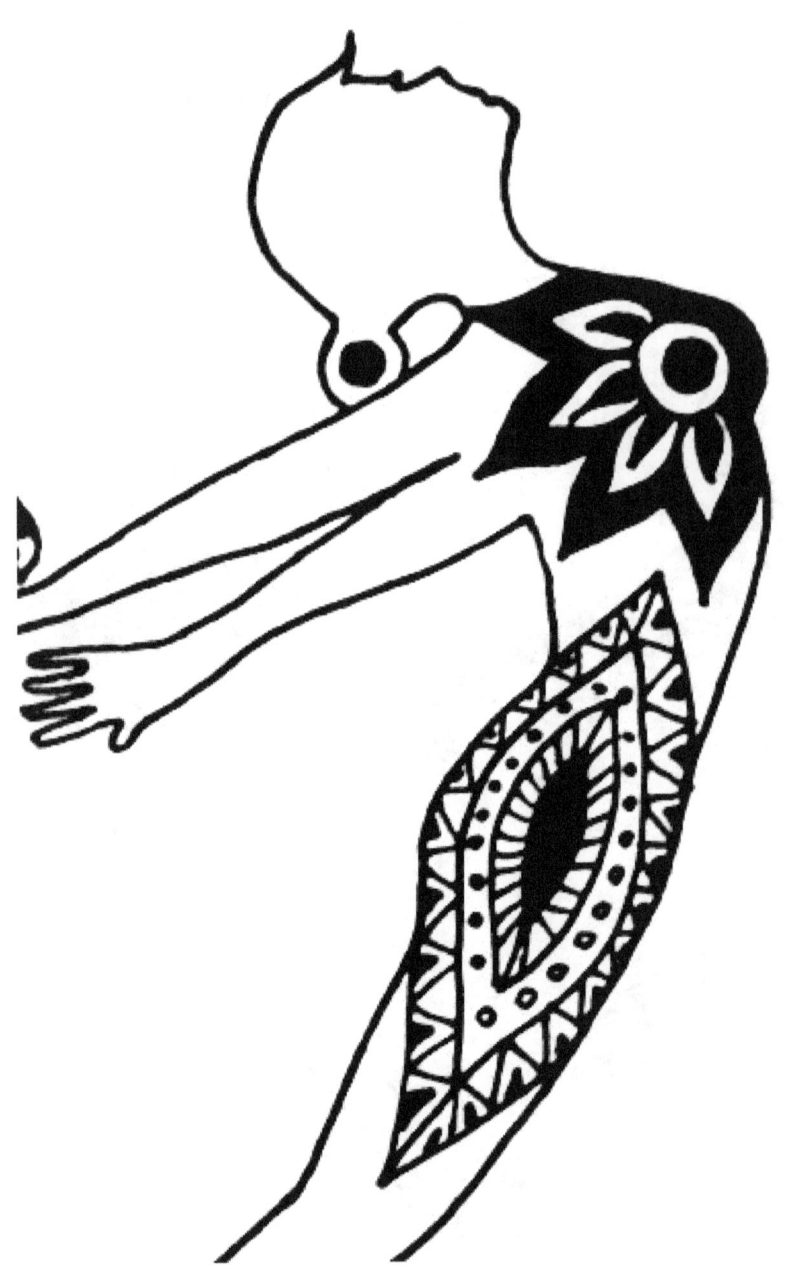

Step 6

Connecting the leaf in the upper portion of the leg of the female, draw an inverted drop and fill it up with ink. As we did in case of the leaf, draw two concentric drops surrounding the first one and fill the last one with dots.
In the remaining portion of the leg, draw some parallel curved lines and fill them with ink alternatively.

Just as you drew a circle and a triangle in the foot of the male, do the same in the foot of the female.

Draw a small circle in the bun of the female.

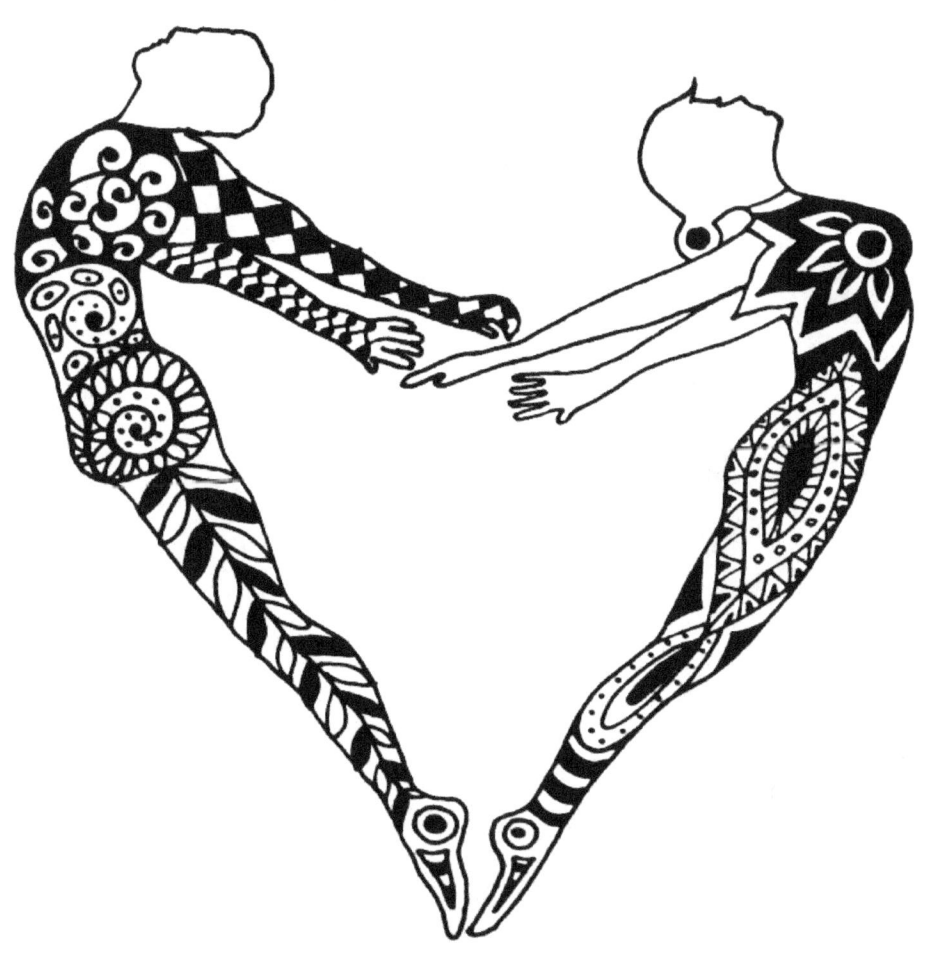

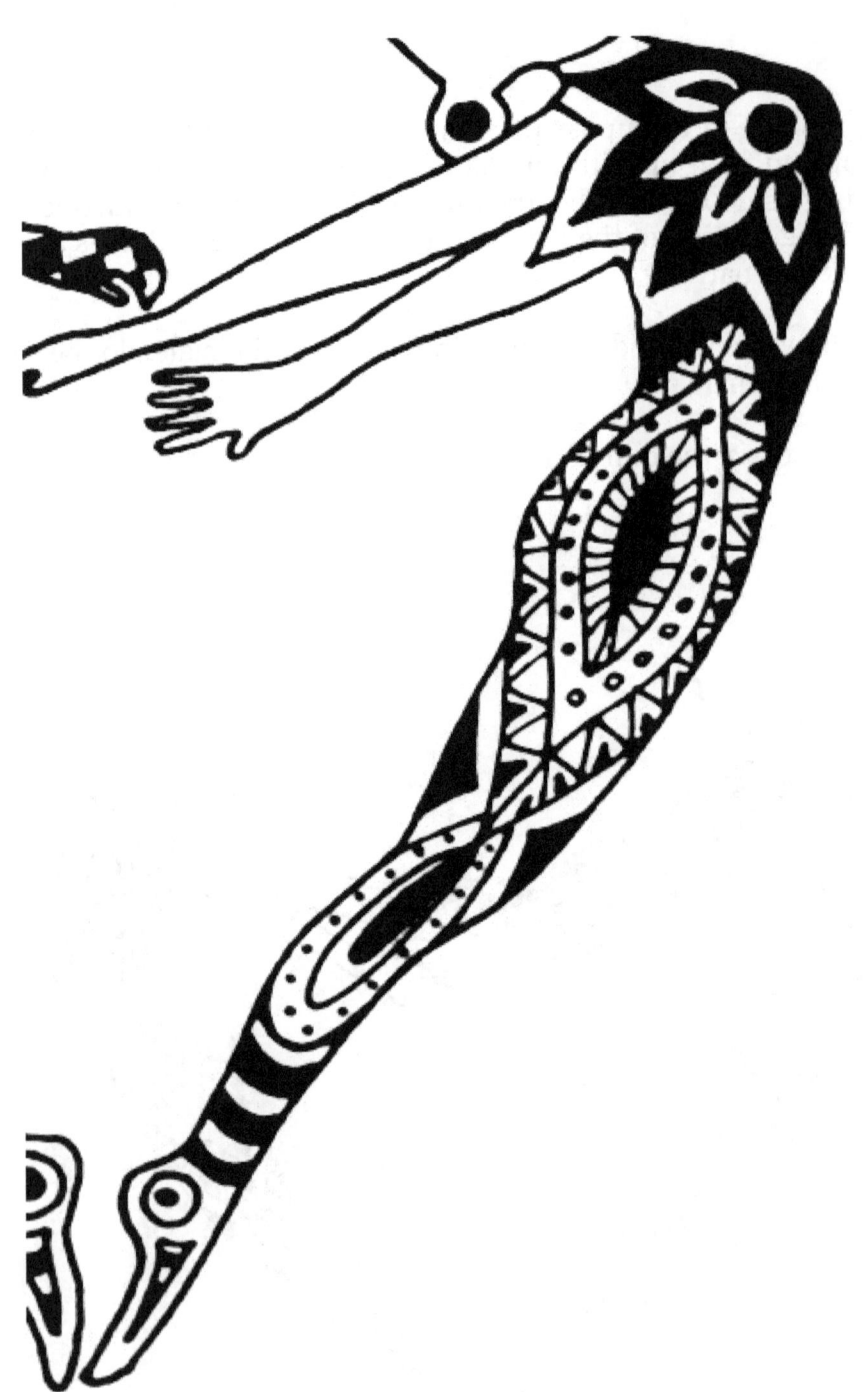

Step 7

Draw a flower in the head of the female and fill the remaining negative area with ink. Fill the arm facing you with eye shaped designs and draw some concentric circles in the other arm. Draw some dots in the hands.

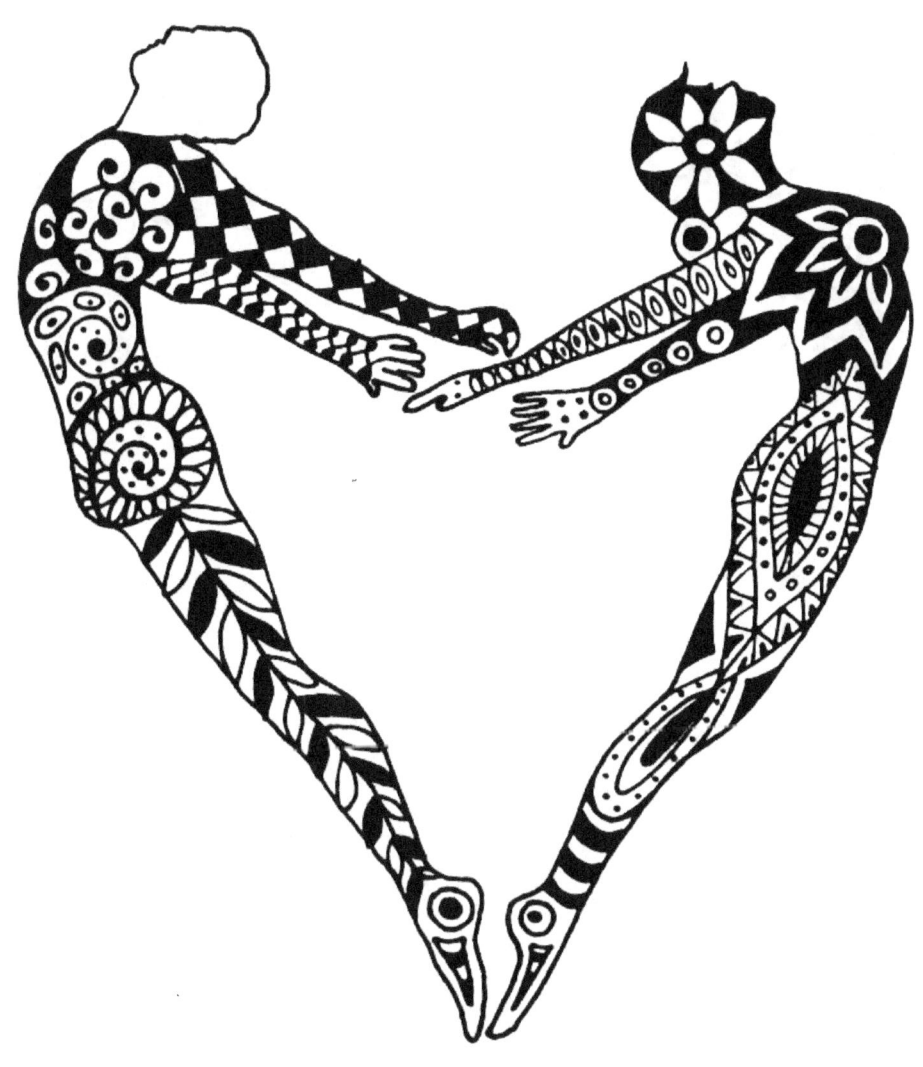

Step 8
Draw an abstract sun design in the head of the male.

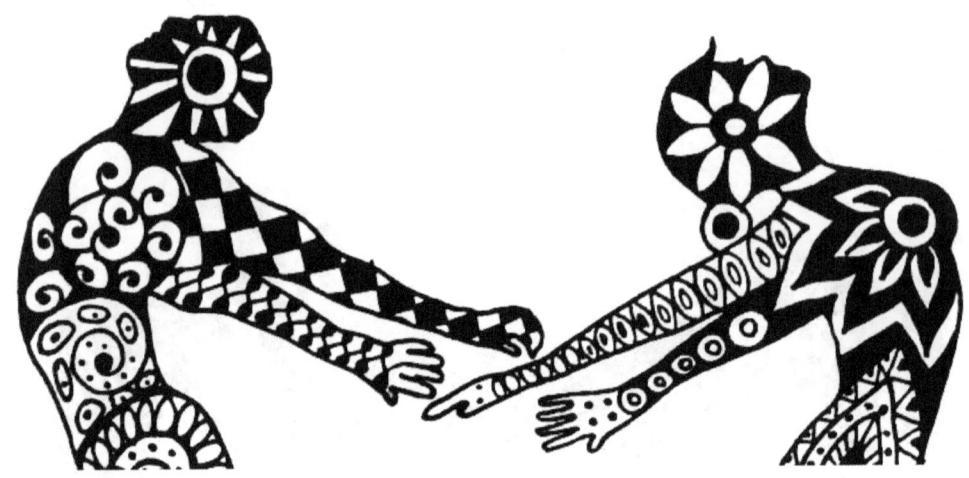

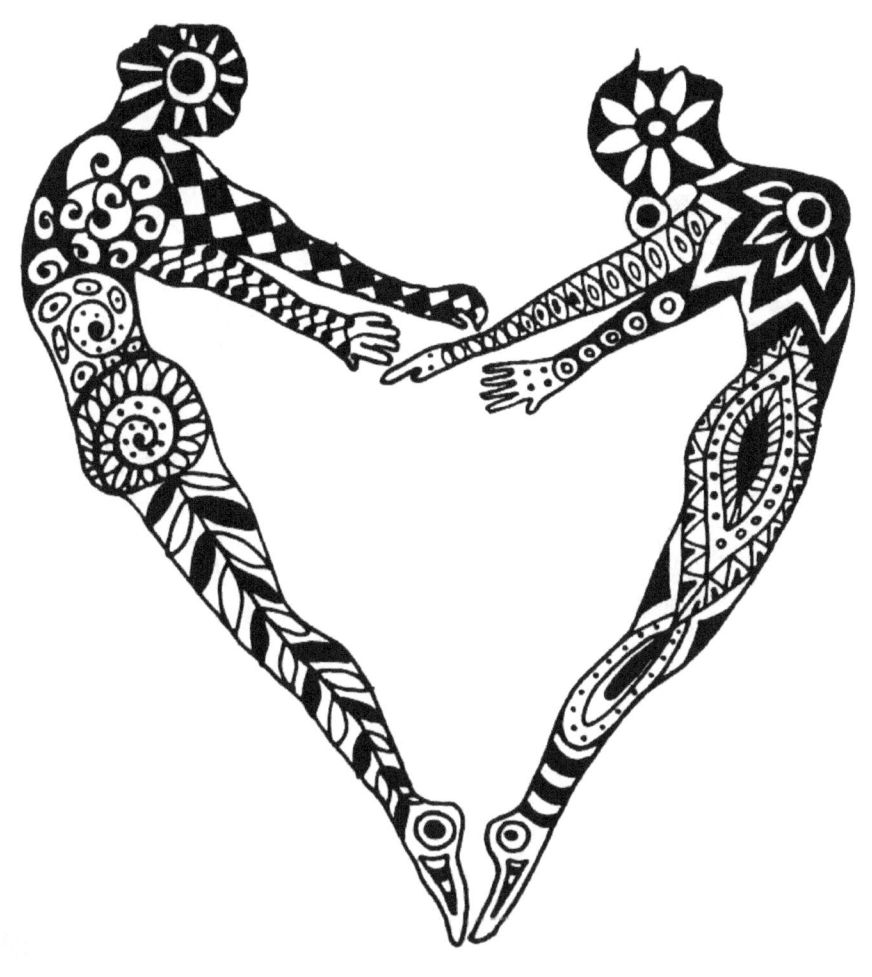

Step 9
Draw some spirals coming out randomly from different areas of the bodies of the dancing couple. Draw sub-stems of the spirals as well.

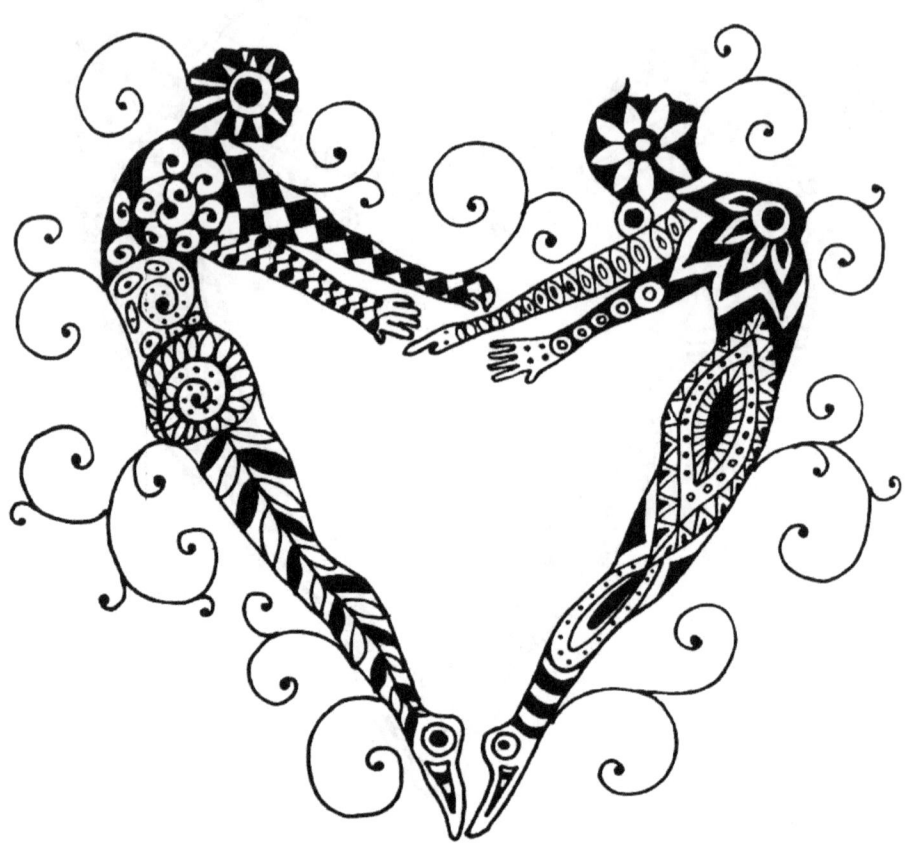

Step 10

Draw some small leaflets coming out from some of the spirals. If you have seen the designs of henna patterns, you would recognize these leaflets instantly. You can make some research for henna patterns to take inspiration for Zen Doodle as well.

Fill up any portions you might have left empty. But remember not to make these drawings overcrowded with designs.

Your first drawing of Zen Doodle dancing heart is complete.

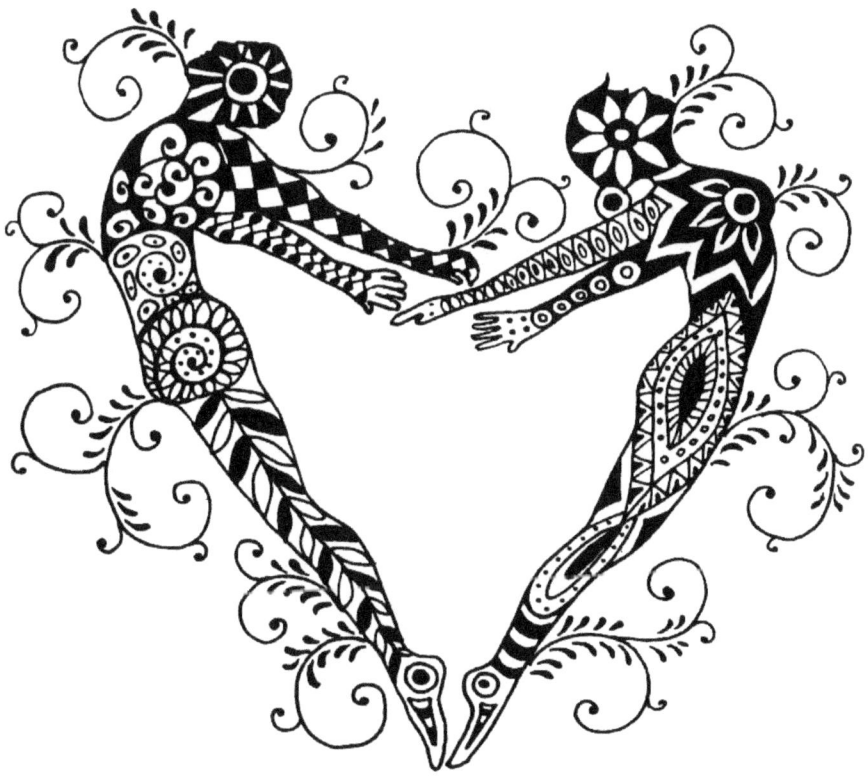

Chapter 2 - Snuggled Couple in a Dance

Draw the outline of a couple snuggled in each other's arms in a ballroom dance pose. Their faces are very close to each other in this intimate position as if they are about to kiss.

Notice that the man is tightly holding the lady at her back and the posture of their bodies should be perfectly drawn accordingly. Even if the facial features are not visible, we can imagine what would be the situation when they were holding each other like that.

Draw some musical notes at the back of the lady's head.

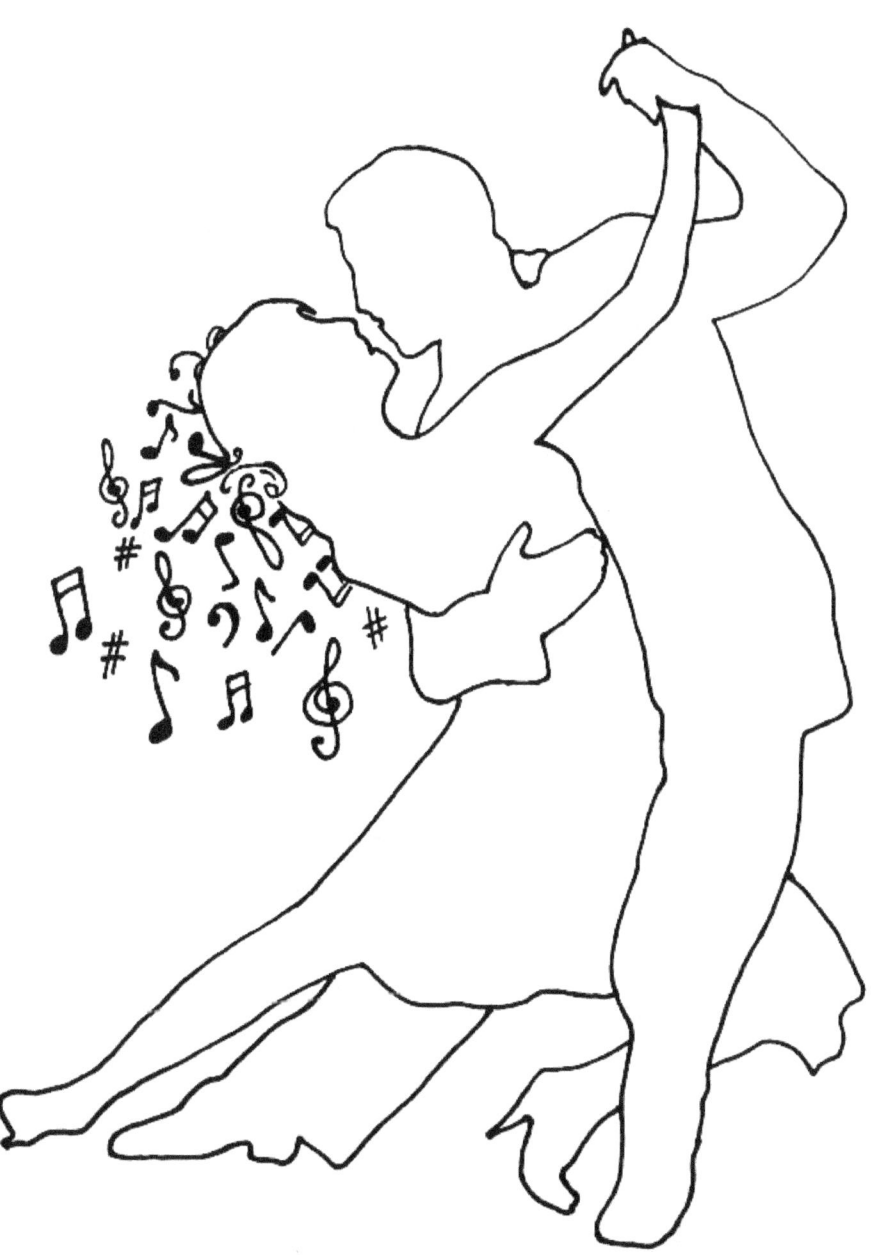

Step 2

Draw a flower each in the head of the male and the female. Cover the remaining negative area around the flower with ink.

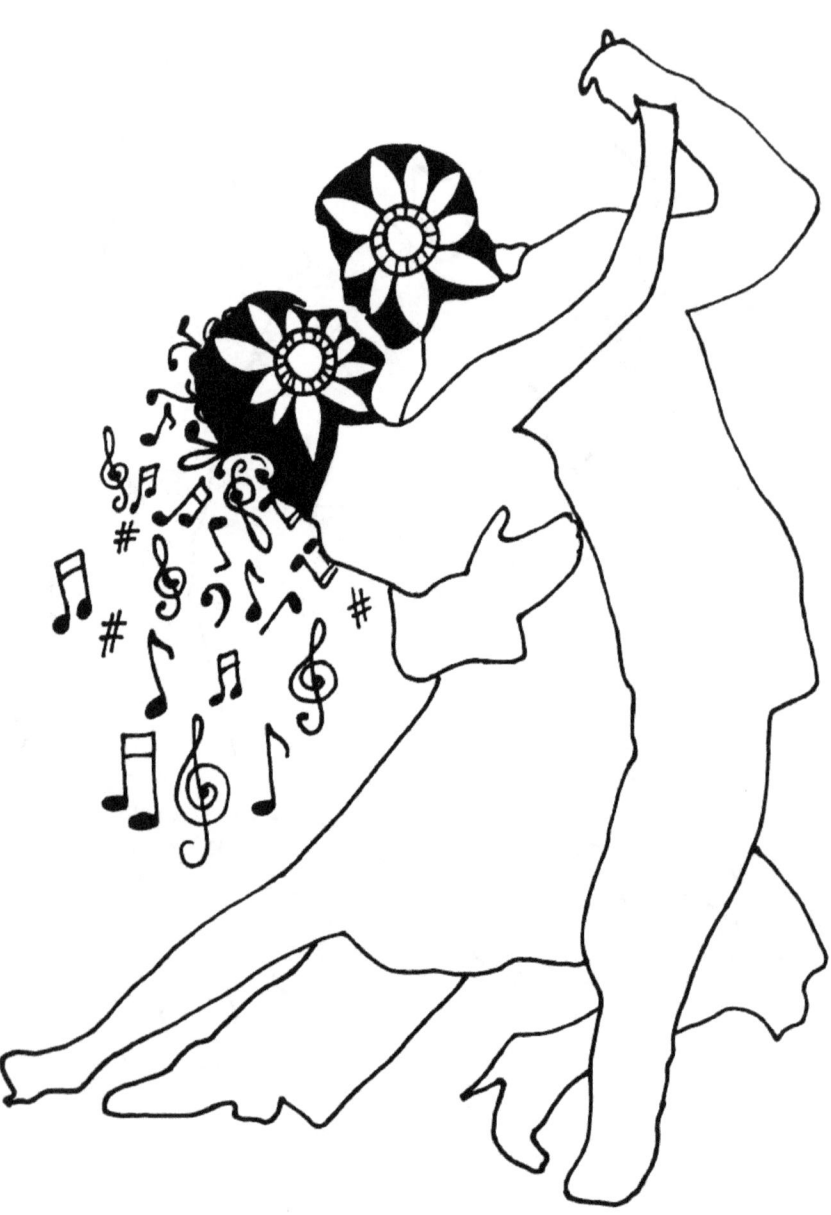

Step 3
Draw zigzag pattern in the right arm of the lady. Draw a triangle in every portion of the design and fill it up with ink.

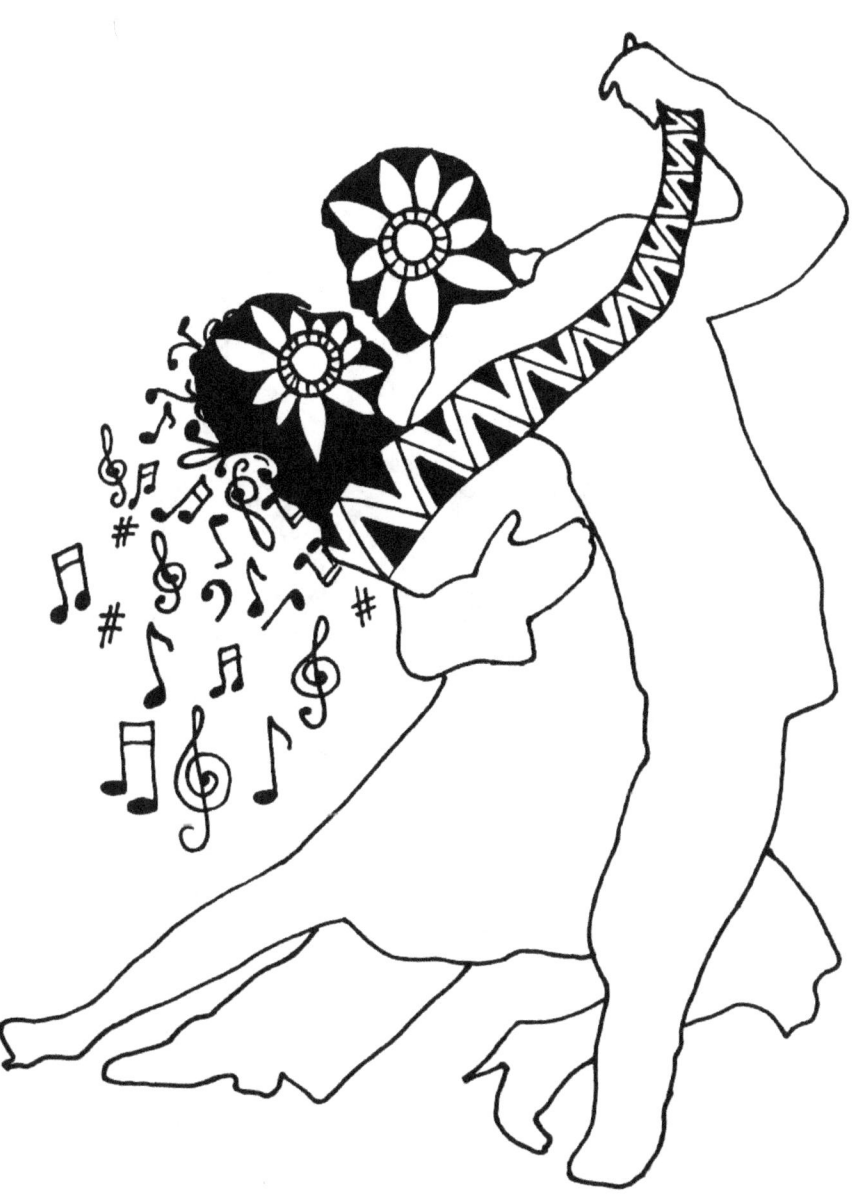

Step 4

Darken the outline of the arm of the lady and the line that is overlapping the man's body. This is done to differentiate the bodies of the couple from each other.

Draw two drop shapes in the body of the man as shown below. Make a leaf like veins in the upper drop and fill up the other with ink. Draw some concentric drops around each drop and draw a few circles (hollow and solid respectively) in the boundary as shown in the picture.

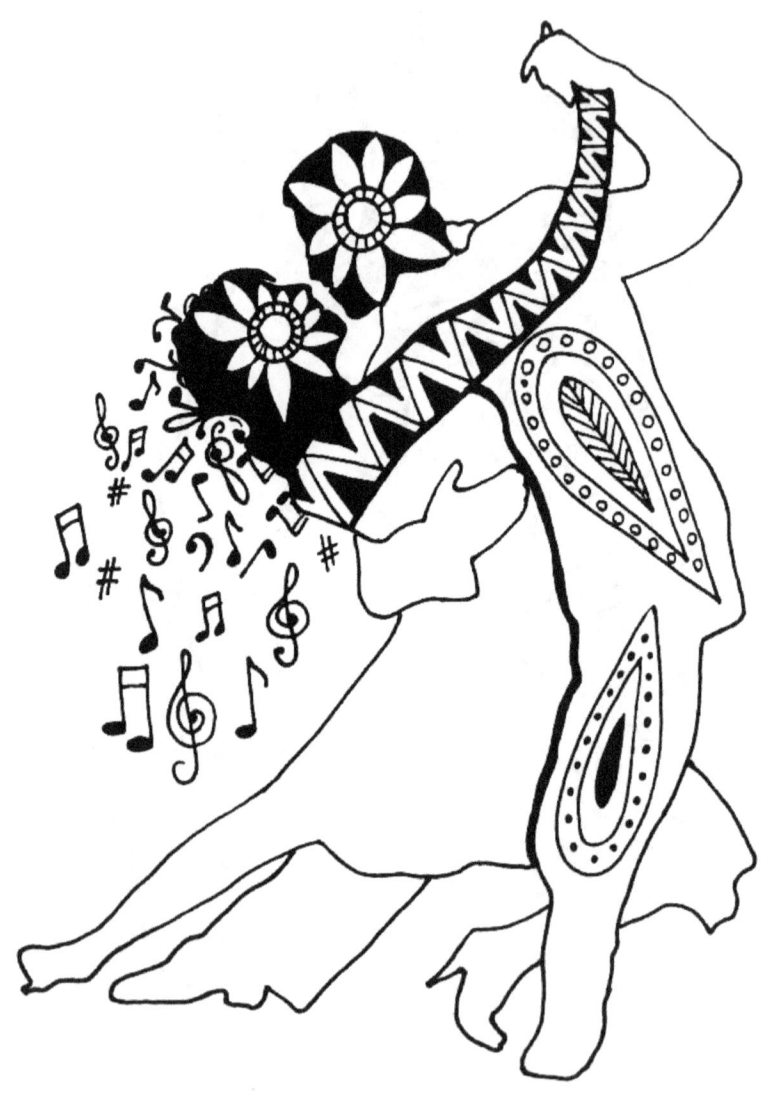

Step 5

The drops in the man's body have to be elaborated more in this step. Draw one more concentric drop shape and make vertical lines to fill up the area. Do not exceed the drop shapes beyond the body of the man. Draw a triangle near the left arm of the man and make a small design in it as shown in the picture.

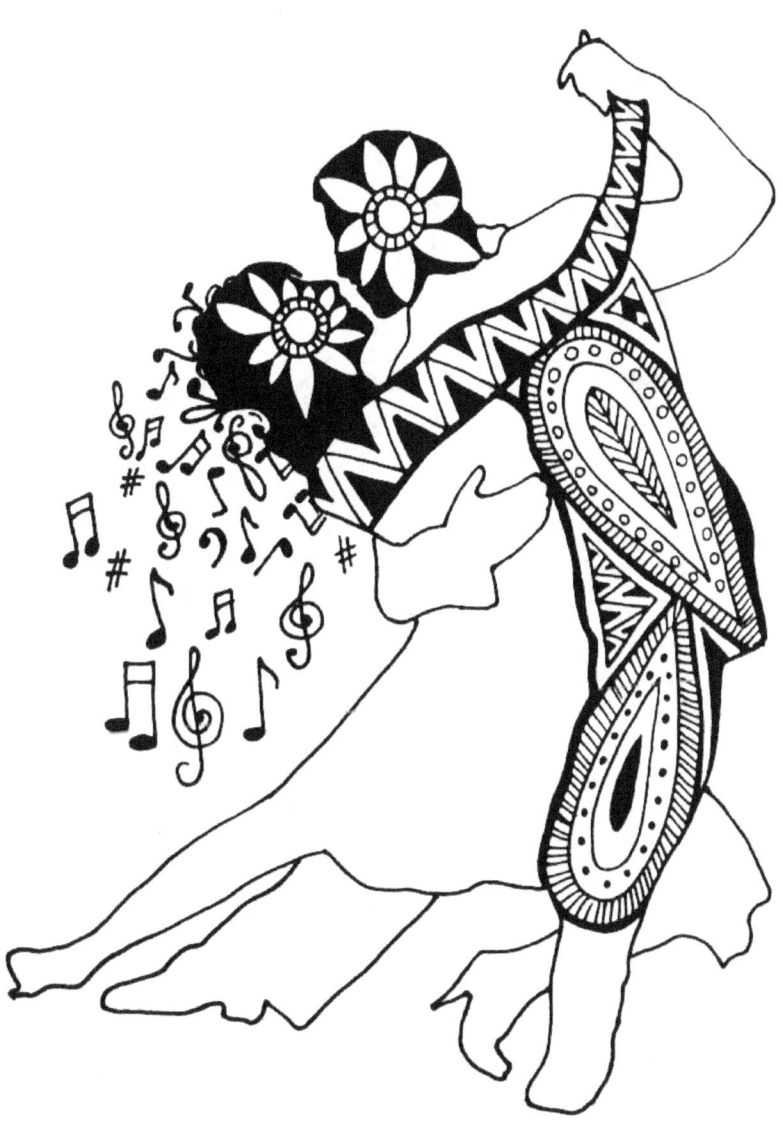

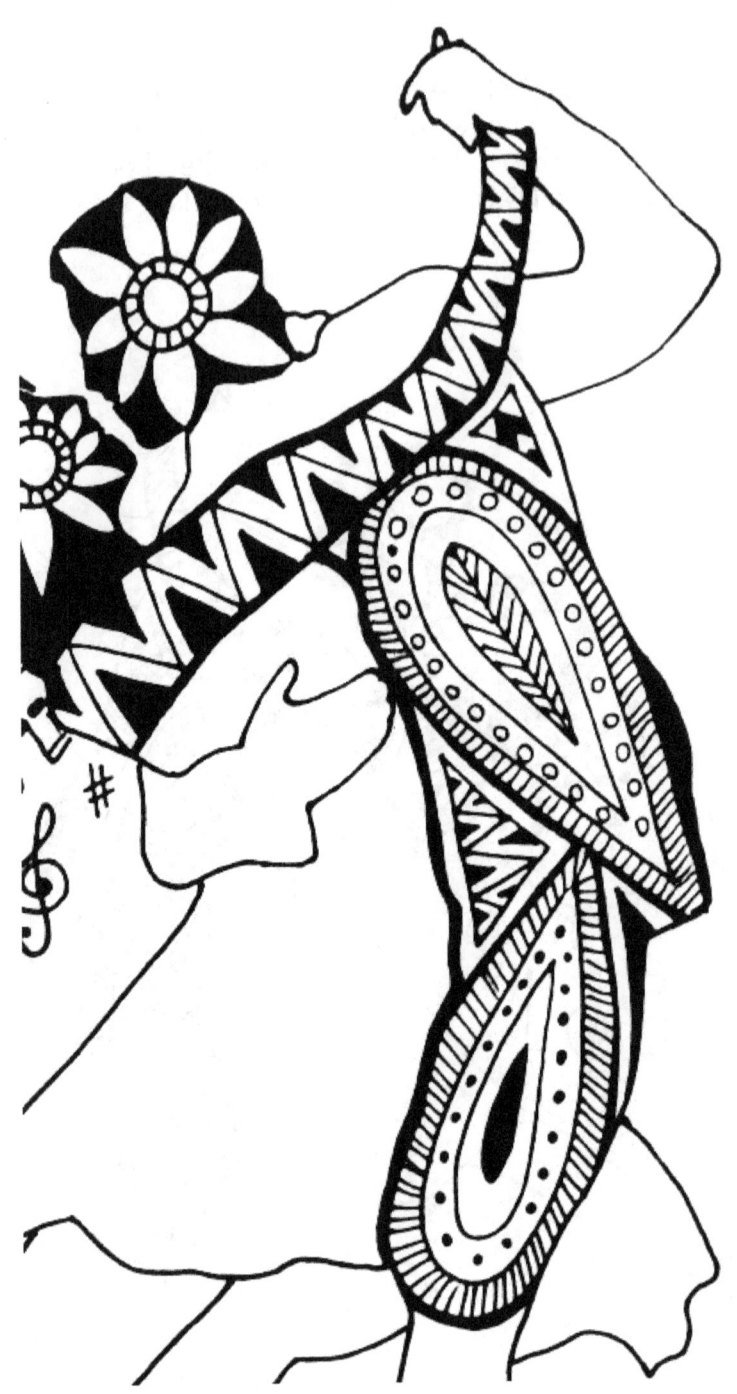

Step 6

Draw loops resembling the shape of "8" below the neck of the man. Draw some concentric ovals in his arm and fill up the negative area with ink.

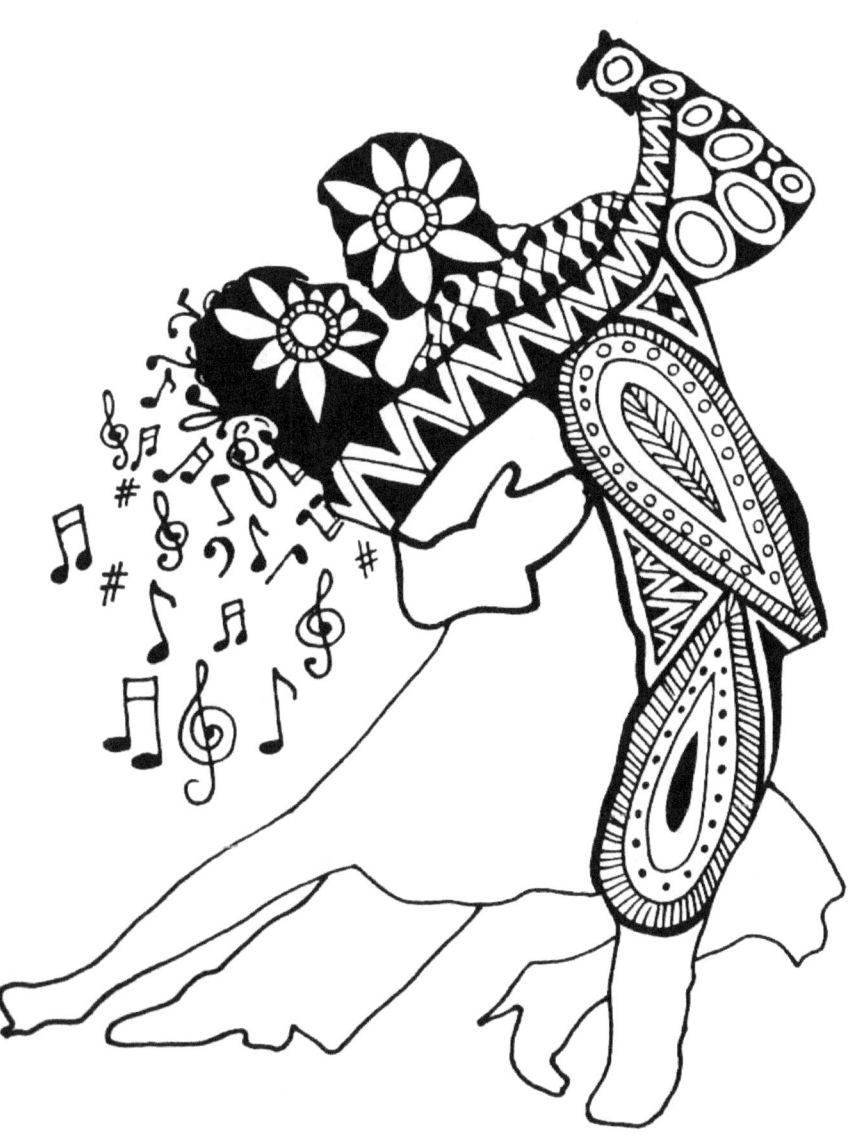

Step 7

Draw large sized scallops in the lady's lower body and color them as shown in the picture.

Draw scallops in the skirt of the lady which is shown behind the man's leg. Draw vertical lines in them as shown.

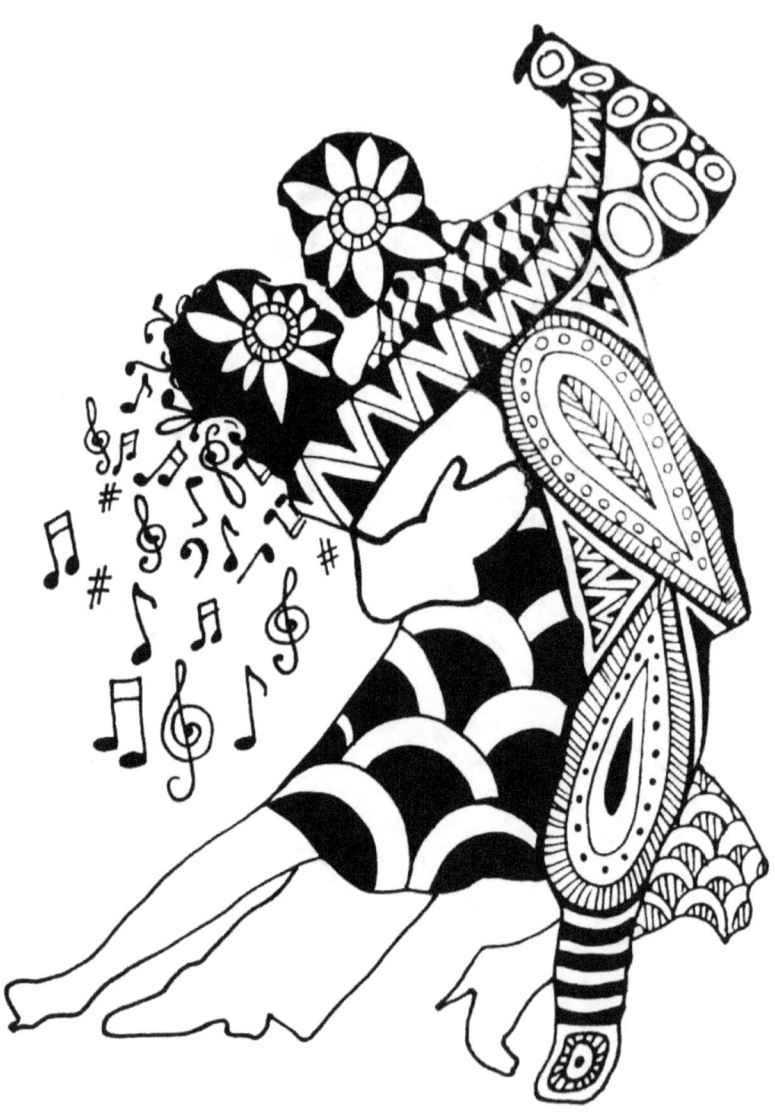

Step 8

Draw the patterns as shown in the legs of the couple. Draw zigzag pattern in the arm of the man at the lady's back.

Fill up any remaining portions in the drawing and your drawing of a couple in a dance is complete.

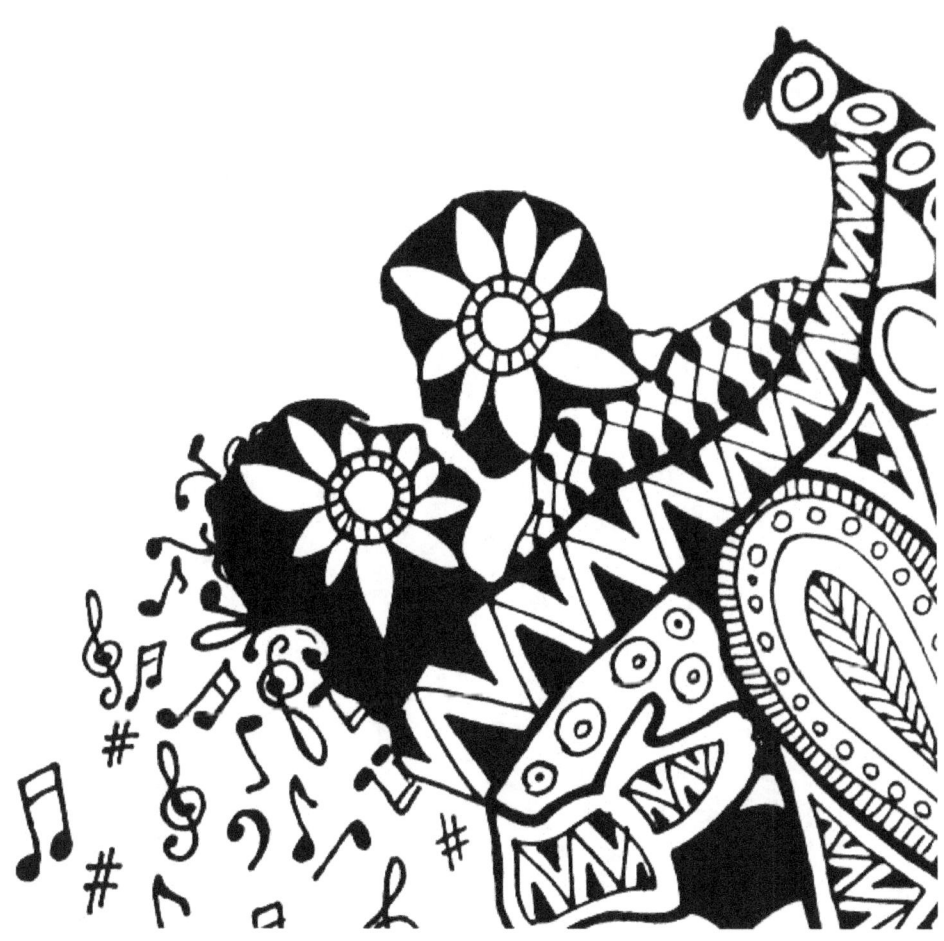

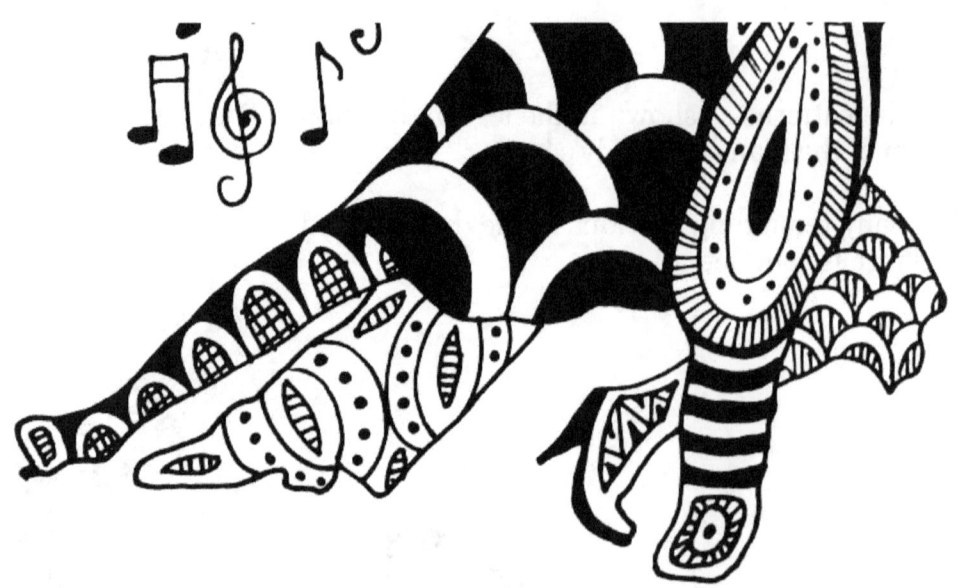

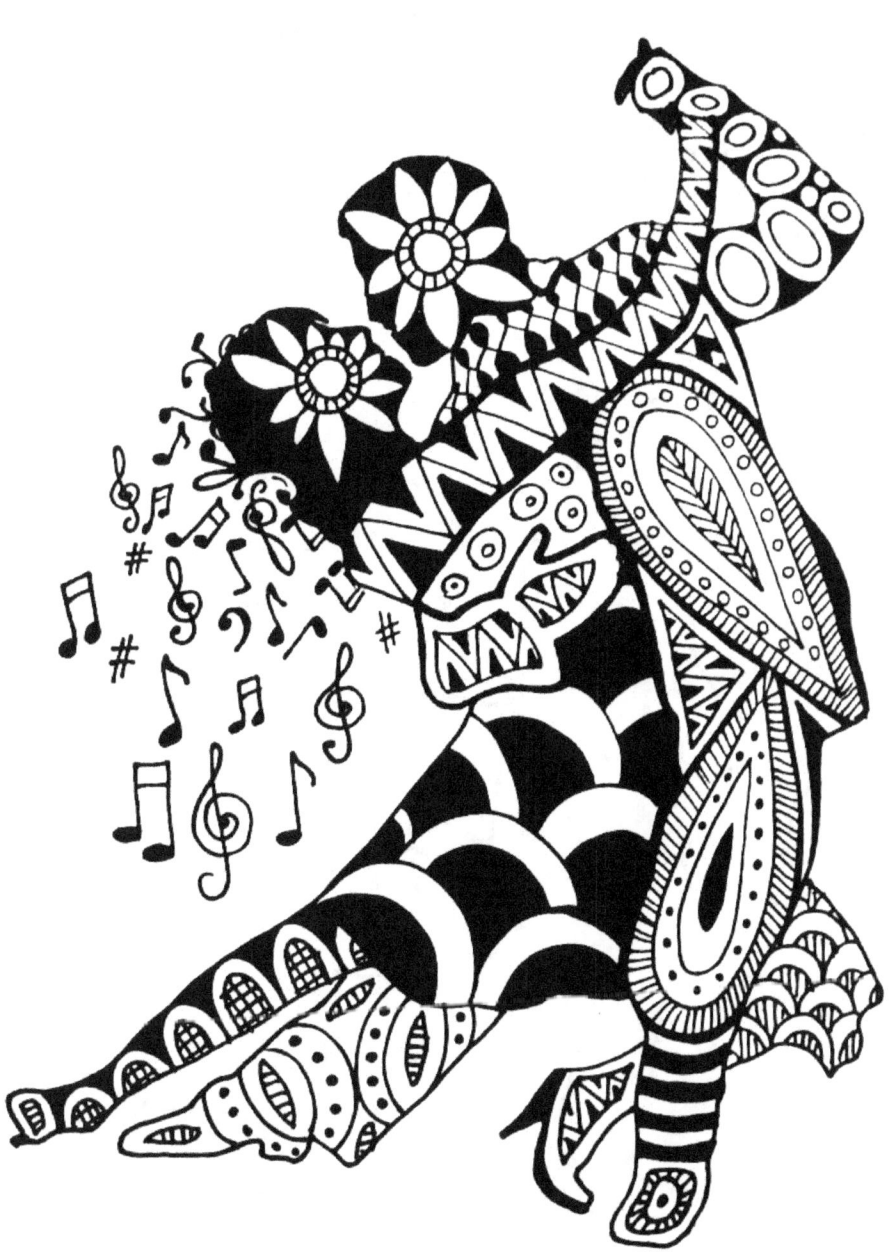

Chapter 3 - Frail Old Couple

Step 1

Draw a frail old couple, the lady walking behind the man and holding his hand. The man is walking with the help of a stick and the lady is carrying a bag in her hand.

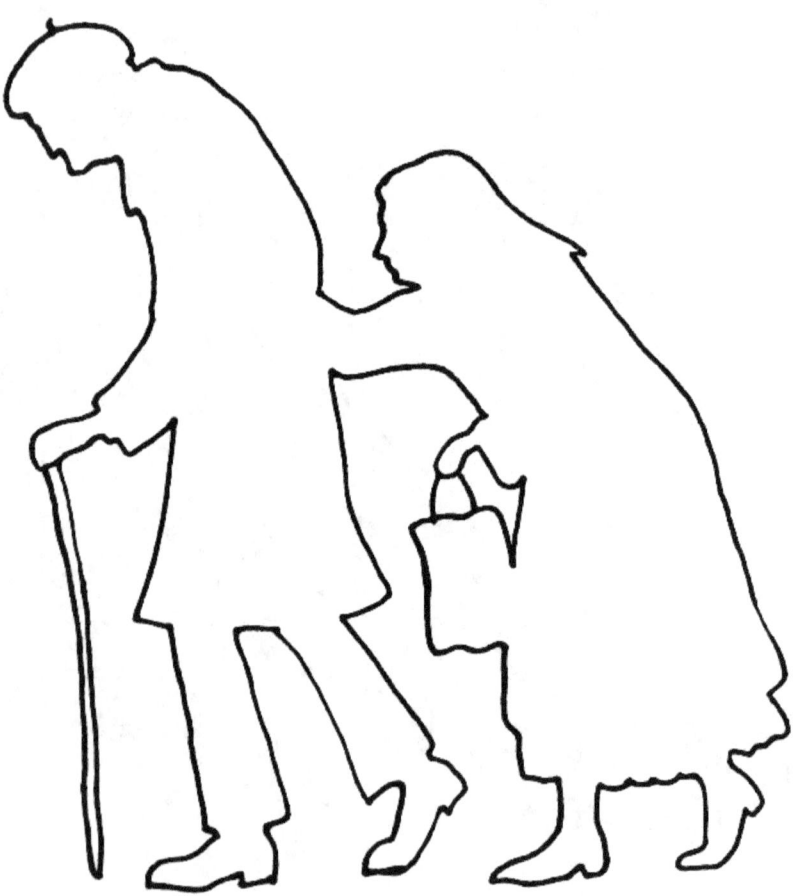

Step 2

Draw a partial flower in the head of the man. Draw a cap on the head and draw a pattern like that of an umbrella in the cap. Draw scallops in the lower portion of the man's shirt. Draw circles in the boundary of these scallops and fill up the negative portion with ink.

Draw a few leaves in the upper portion of the shirt and surround them with thick boundaries.

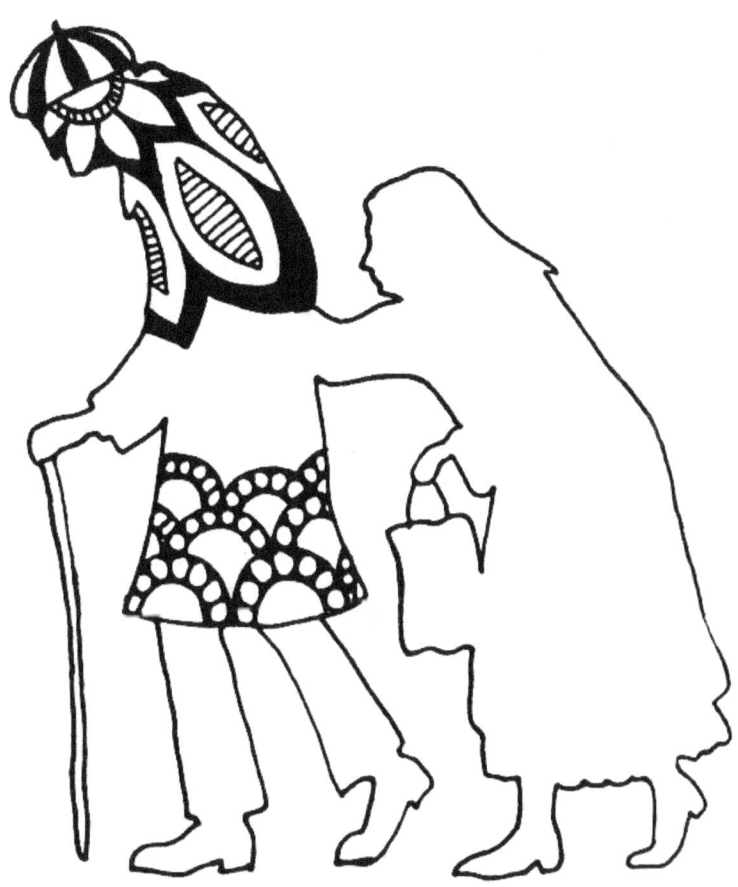

Step 3
Draw a pattern of checks in one leg of the man and double zigzag pattern in the form of crisscross in the other leg.

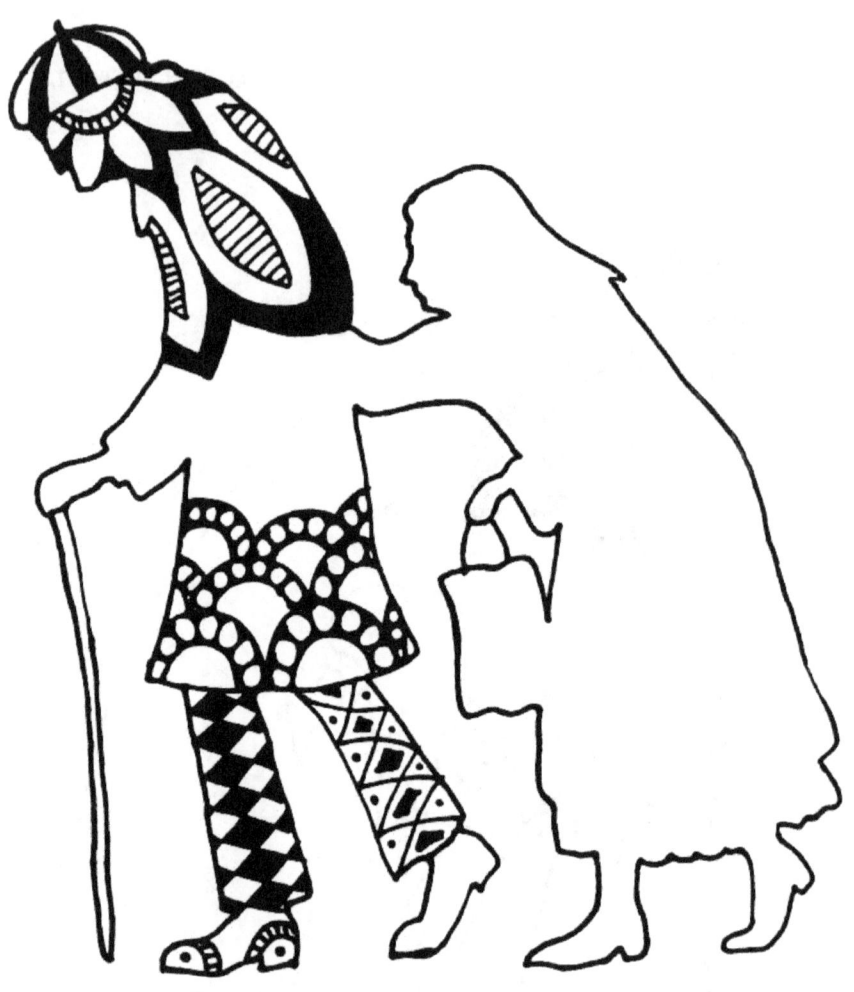

Step 4

Draw eye-shaped designs starting from the arm of the man till the arm of the lady. It depicts the union and the strong bond of the old couple. Below the arm of the man, draw a semi-circle like pattern as shown in the picture. Draw two semi-circles in the feet.

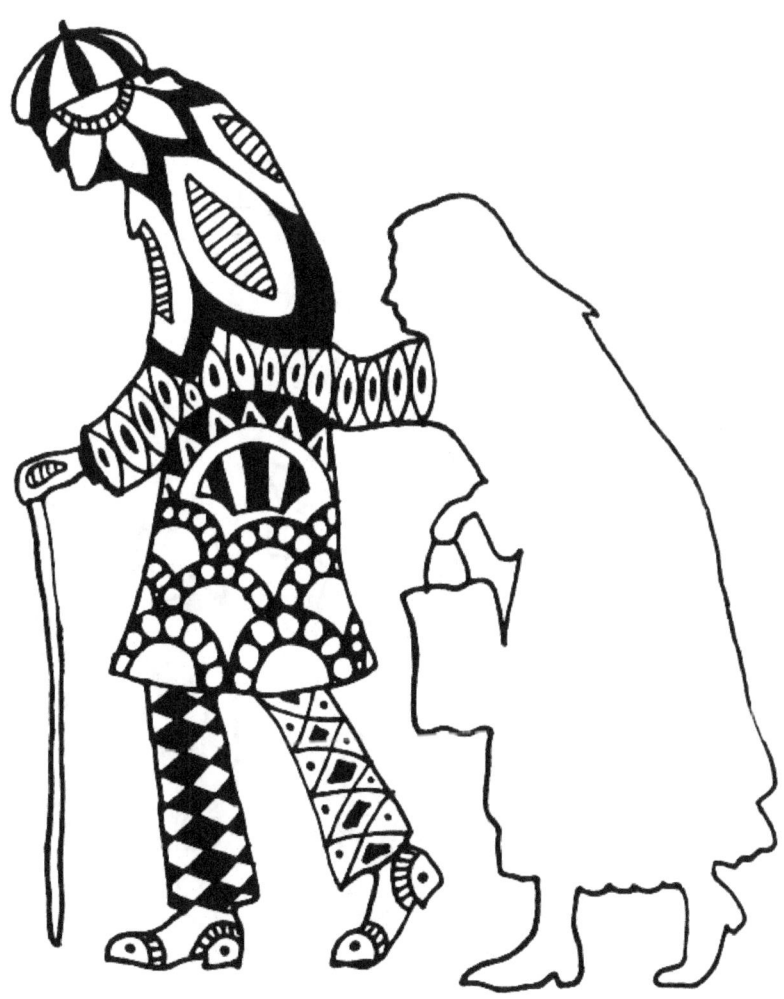

Step 5
Draw a large flower in the dress of the lady. Draw scallops in the lower margin of the dress.

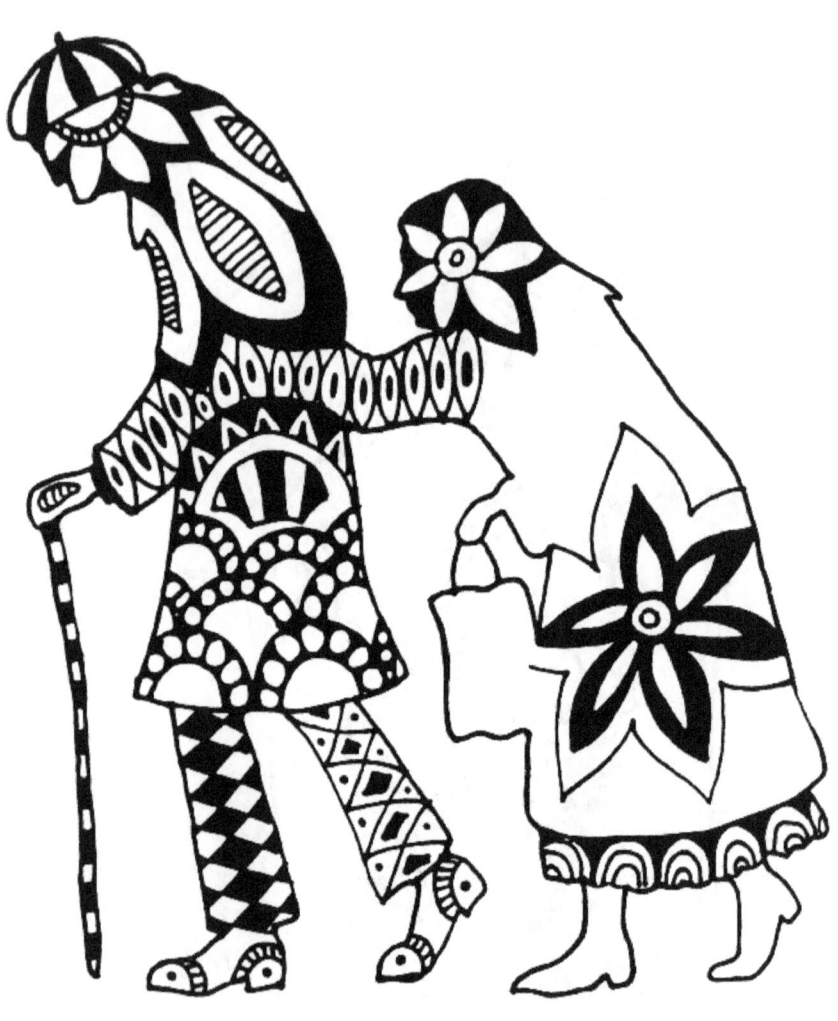

Step 6

Draw patterns of vertical lines around the flower in the dress of the lady as shown in the picture. Draw two inverted drops near the shoulders and surround them with some hollow and solid small circles. Complete the feet of the lady with the drawings of semi-circles and small circles.

Your drawing of a Zen Doodle frail old couple is complete.

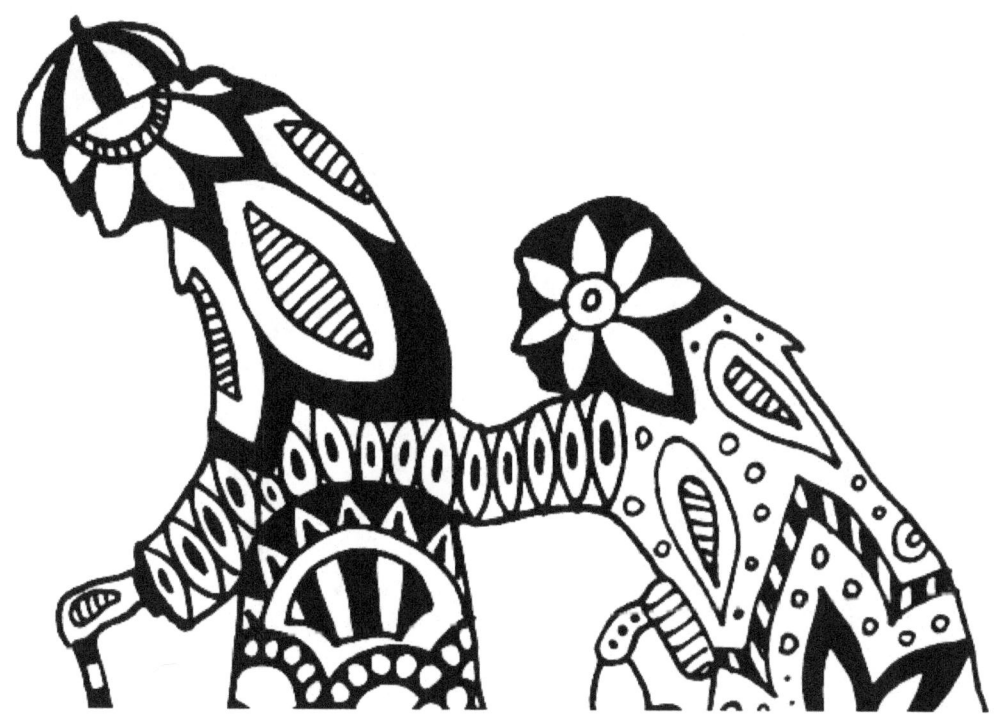

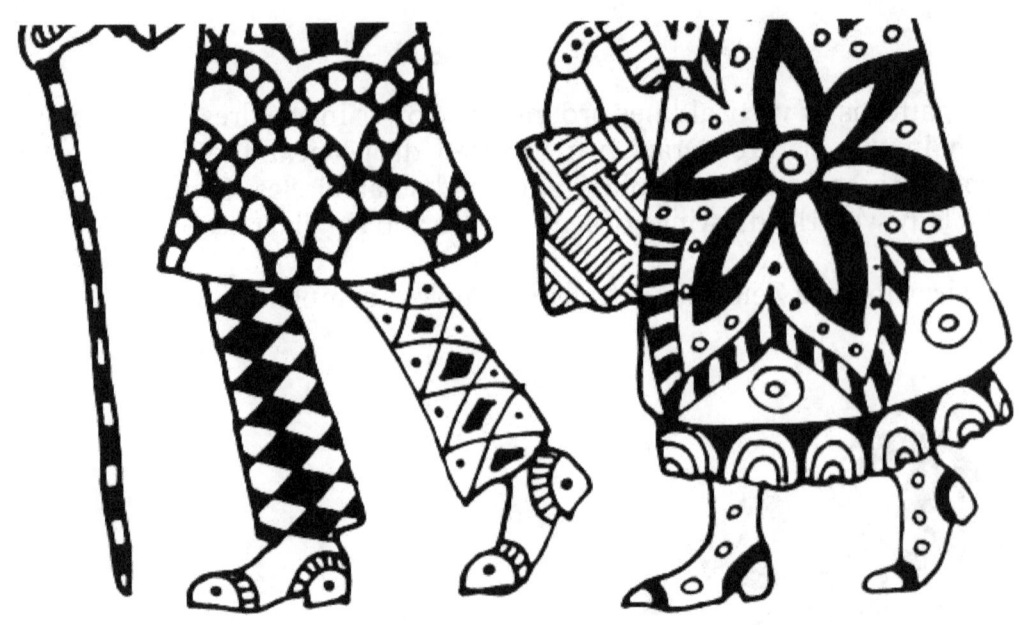

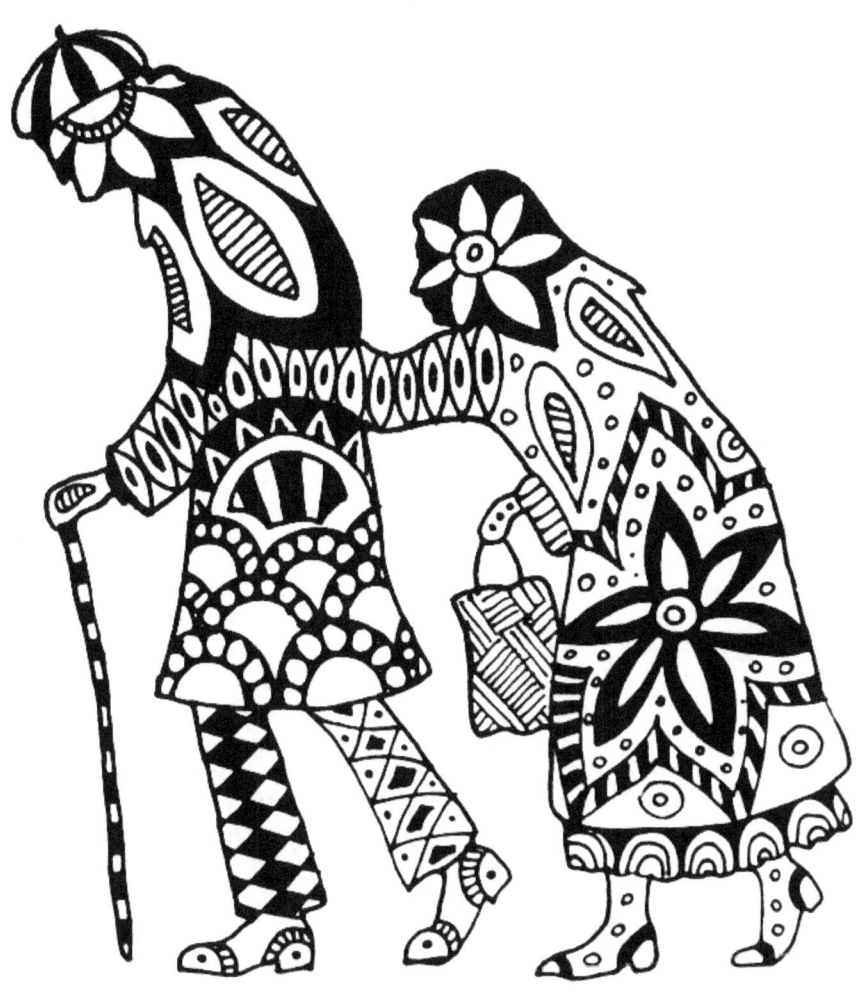

Chapter 4 - Family at a Walk

Step 1
Draw the outline of the family at a walk, a father, a mother and a child. The child is holding hands with both the parents.

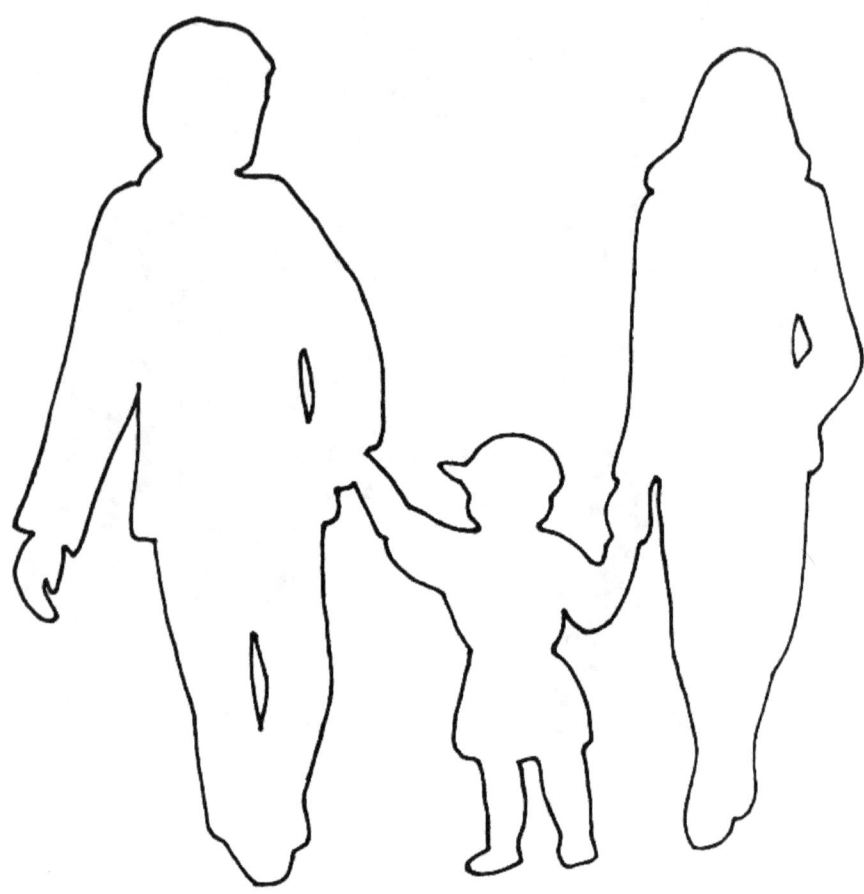

Step 2

Below the neck of the father, draw some broad U-shaped lines and fill the margins with zigzag pattern. Draw a triangle in each space of this pattern. In the second space, draw some bullets and surround them with circles. Draw scallops in the lower portion of the shirt. Fill the arms of the shirt with patterns as shown in the picture.

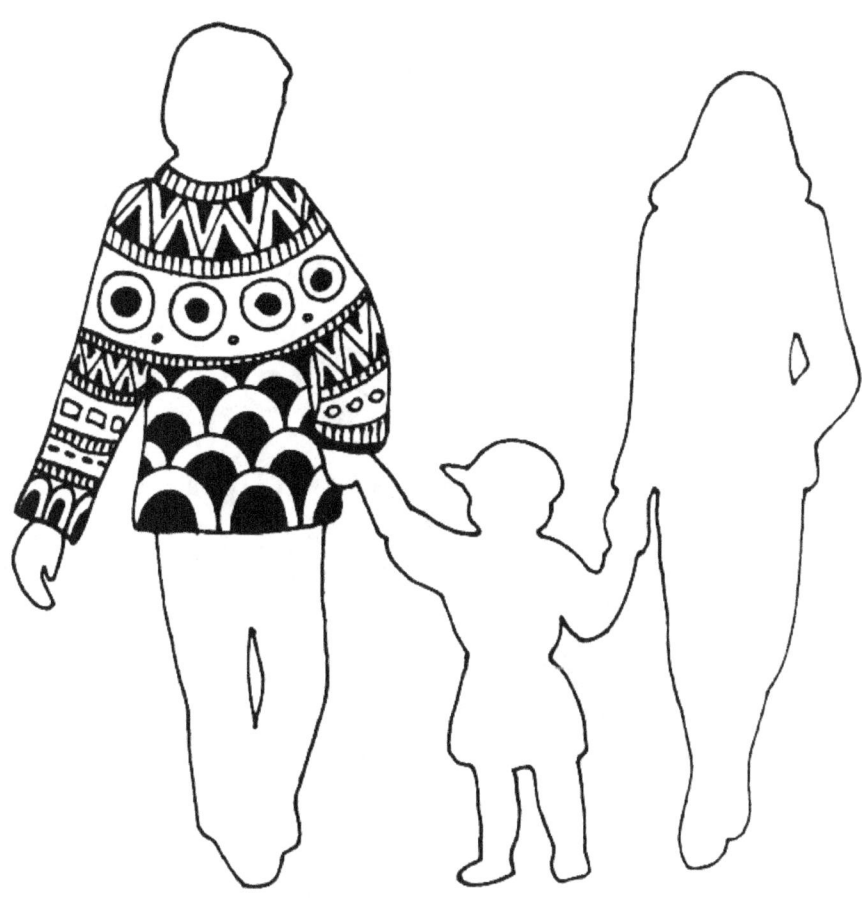

Step 3

Draw large triangles with parallel outlines in the pants of the man and fill them up with vertical lines. In the lower portion of the pants, draw drop shapes and fill them up with smaller drop patterns as illustrated. Draw U-shaped design in the feet and fill them with parallel vertical lines.

In the head, draw a partial flower in the lower right side and fill the remaining head with triangles and circles as shown.

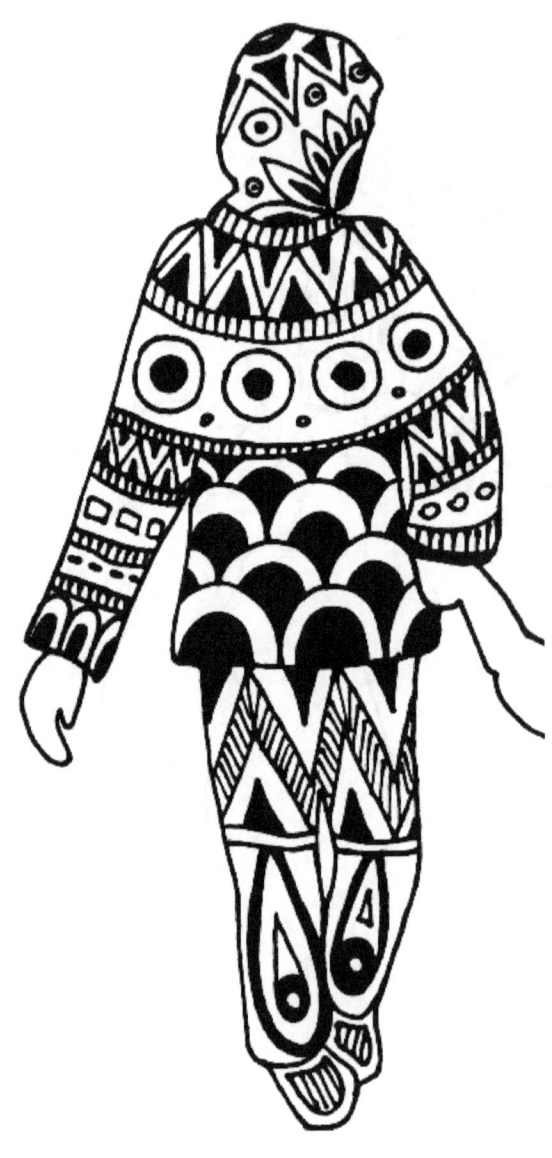

Step 4

In the upper left portion of the mother, draw some drop shaped petal forms and draw some smaller drops and circles as shown in the picture. Draw a large leaf emerging out of the converging point of these petals and highlight its veins. Draw some inverted scallops in the legs.

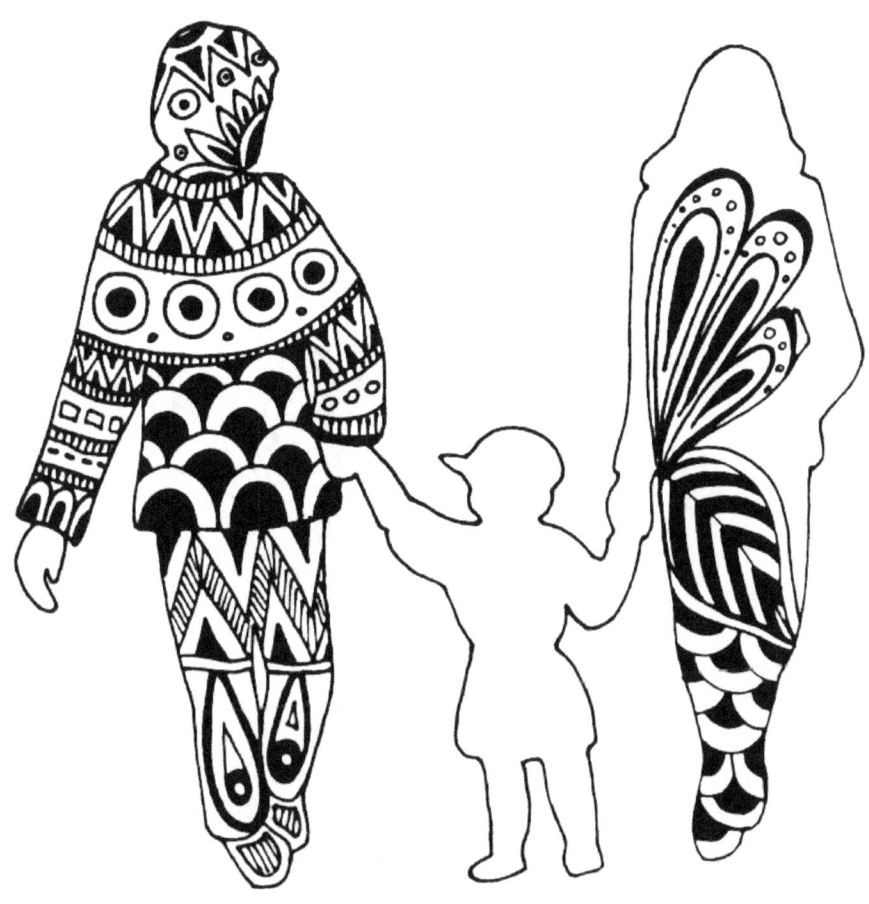

Step 5
Draw some U-shaped designs with parallel outlines in the rightmost side and fill the margins of outlines with spikes. Draw a large flower in the head of the mother.

In the spaces that are remaining, draw some bullets and two drop shapes in the shoulders.

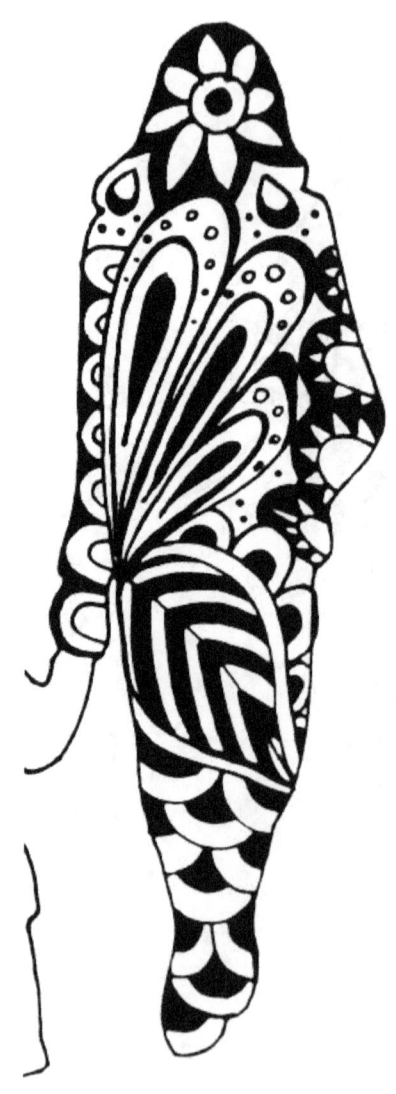

Step 6

Draw a partial flower in the cap of the kid and some U-shapes in the face. Draw a large flower in the chest portion and highlight its outlines.

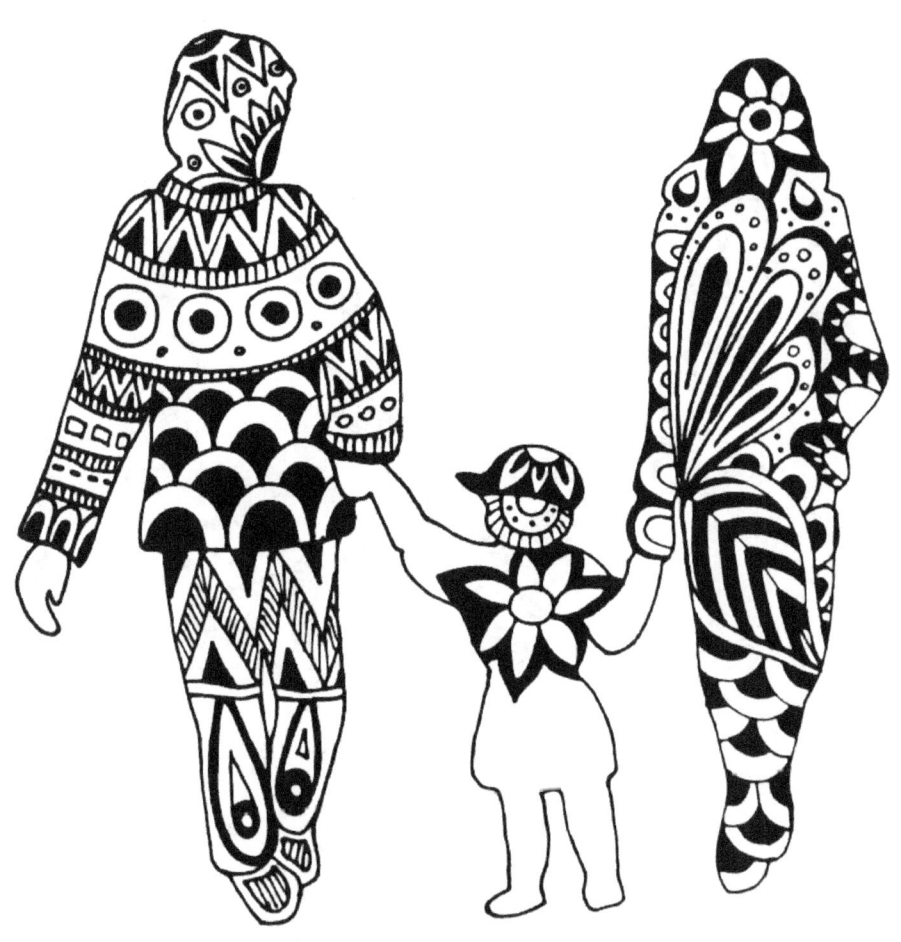

Step 7

Draw two leaves in the lower portion of the kid's shirt. Draw some scallops in the right leg and parallel lines in the left leg. Fill the alternate portions of the left leg with some small bullets.

The drawing of a Zen Doodle family at a walk is complete.

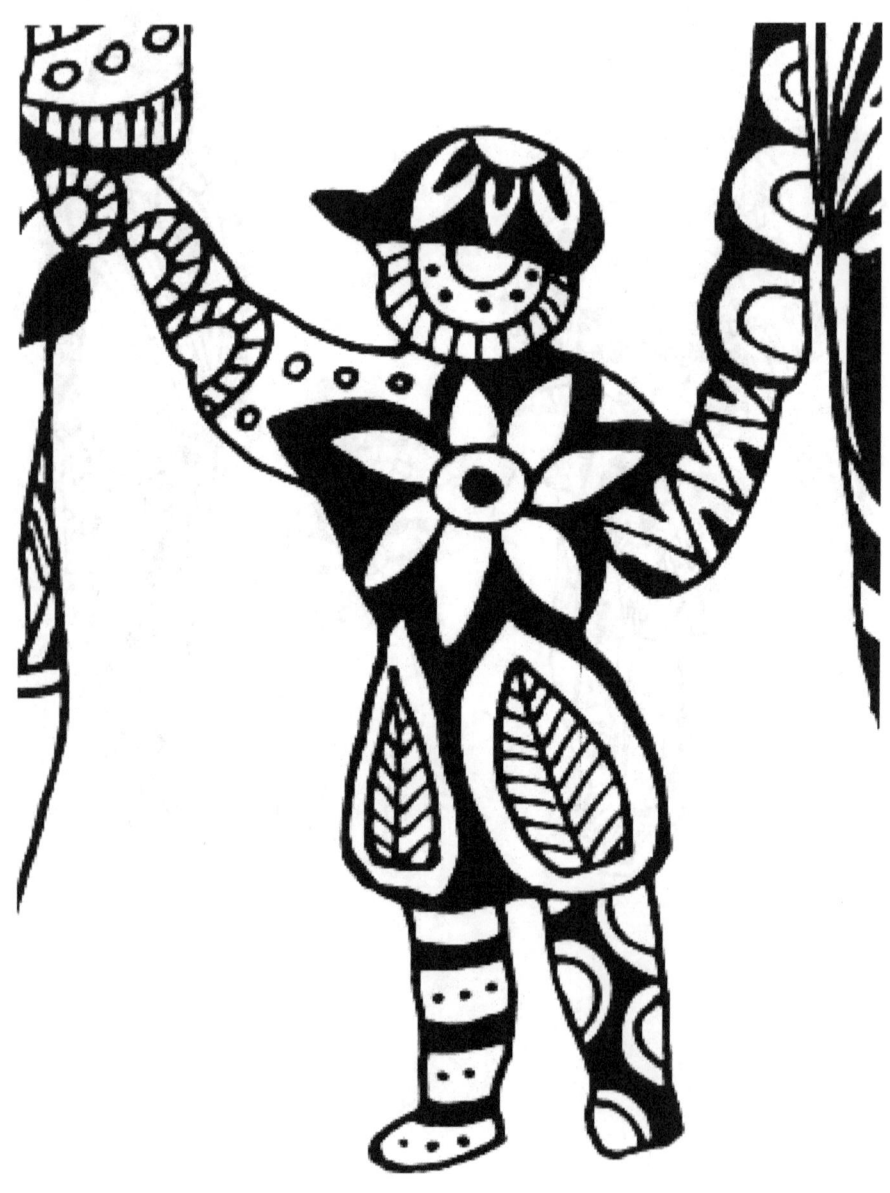

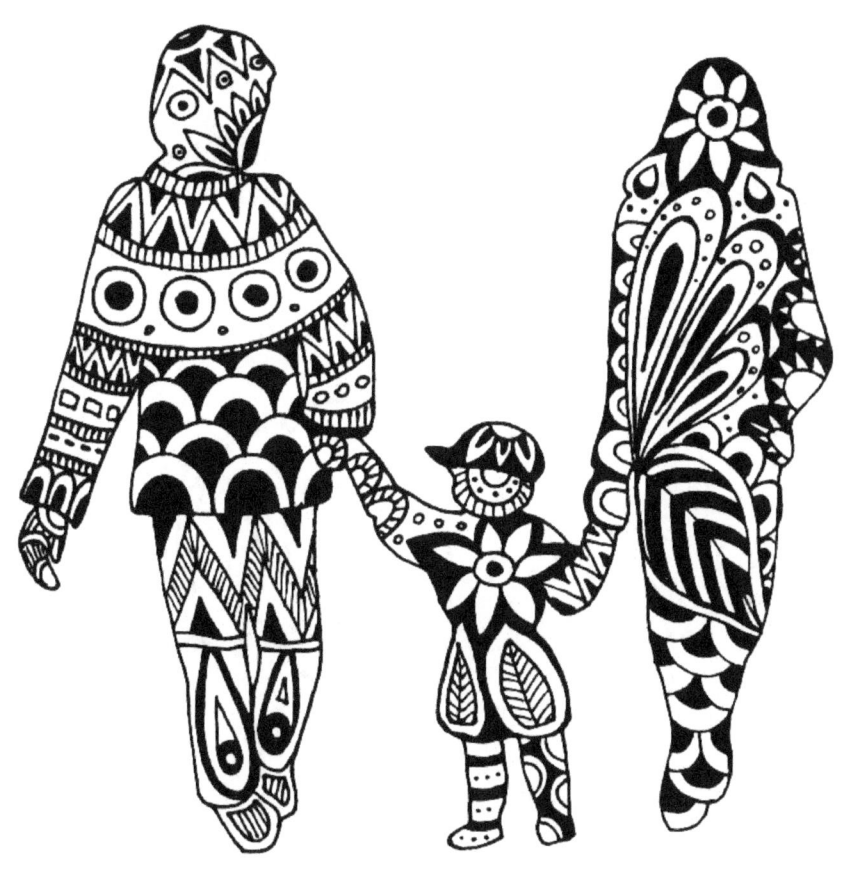

Chapter 5 - Pregnant Lady in the Arms of her Husband

Step 1
Draw the outline of the couple- a pregnant lady with her back hugged to her husband. Their bodies are shown merged with each other to show the union.

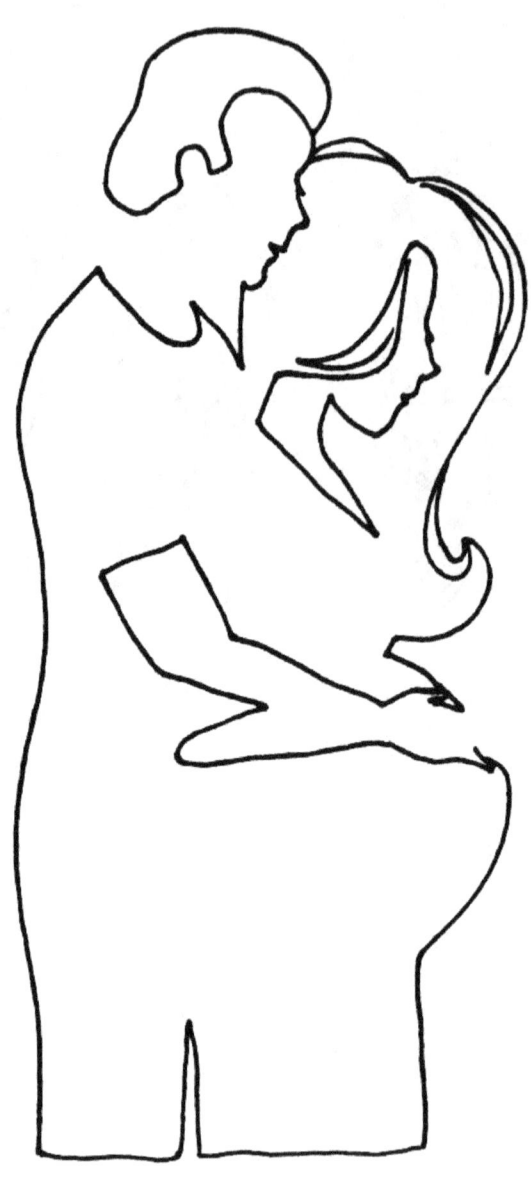

Step 2

Draw a large flower in the belly of the lady. If you can recall, we have drawn such flowers in the heads of the people in the previous illustrations. Here, a baby is residing inside the lady. That is why; we have drawn the same flower in her belly. That is what we call strategic positioning of patterns and designs.

Draw some diagonal parallel lines in the legs of the couple and fill the margins with the patterns as shown in the picture.

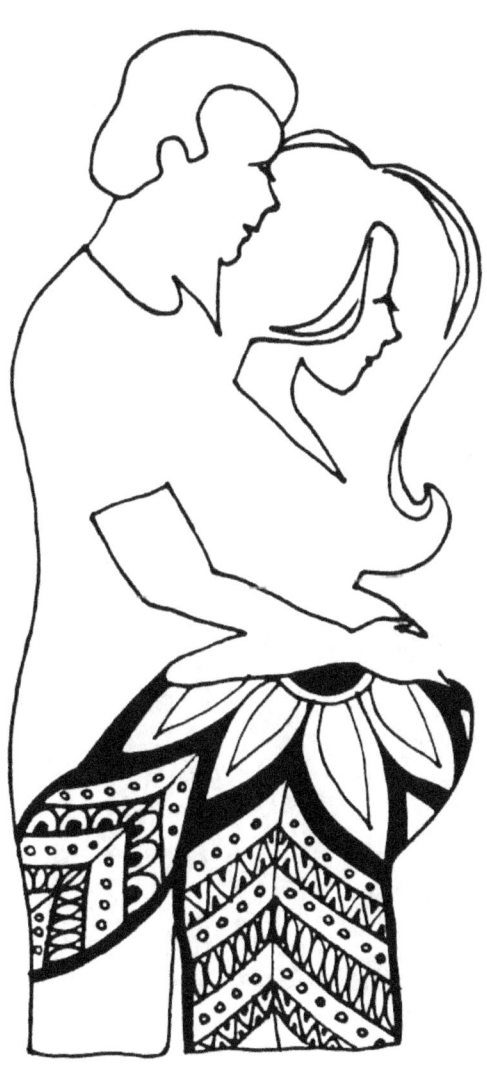

Step 3

Draw some scallops in the legs of the man and the breast portion of the lady. Draw the diagonal lines like we drew in the legs in the waist portion of the man.

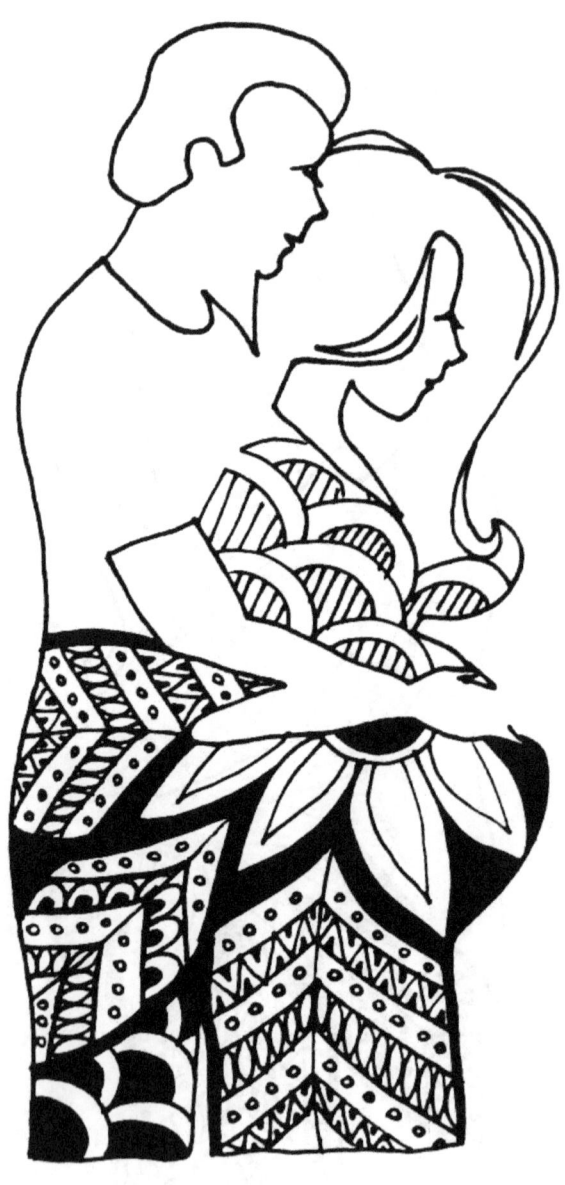

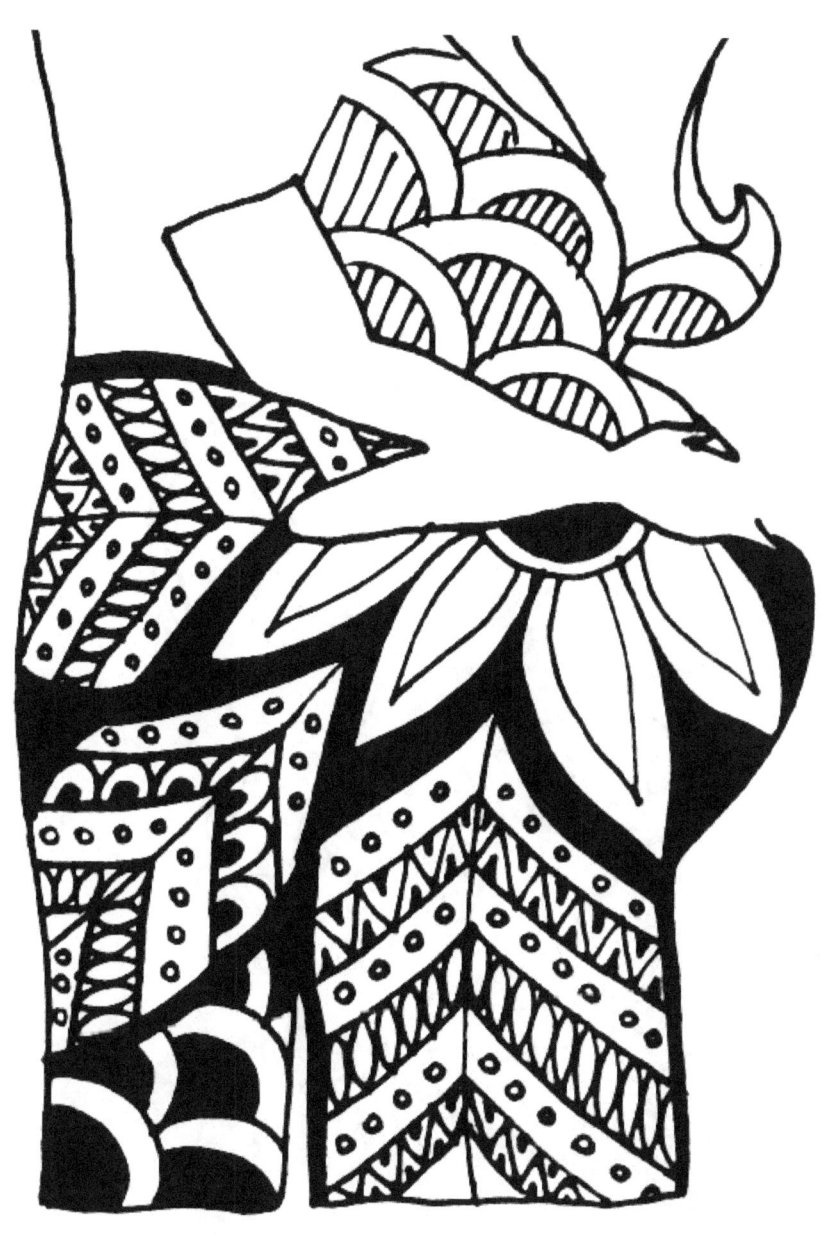

Step 4
Draw a large flower with bold outlines in the shoulder of the man. Draw a small triangle in the sleeve of the man's shirt.

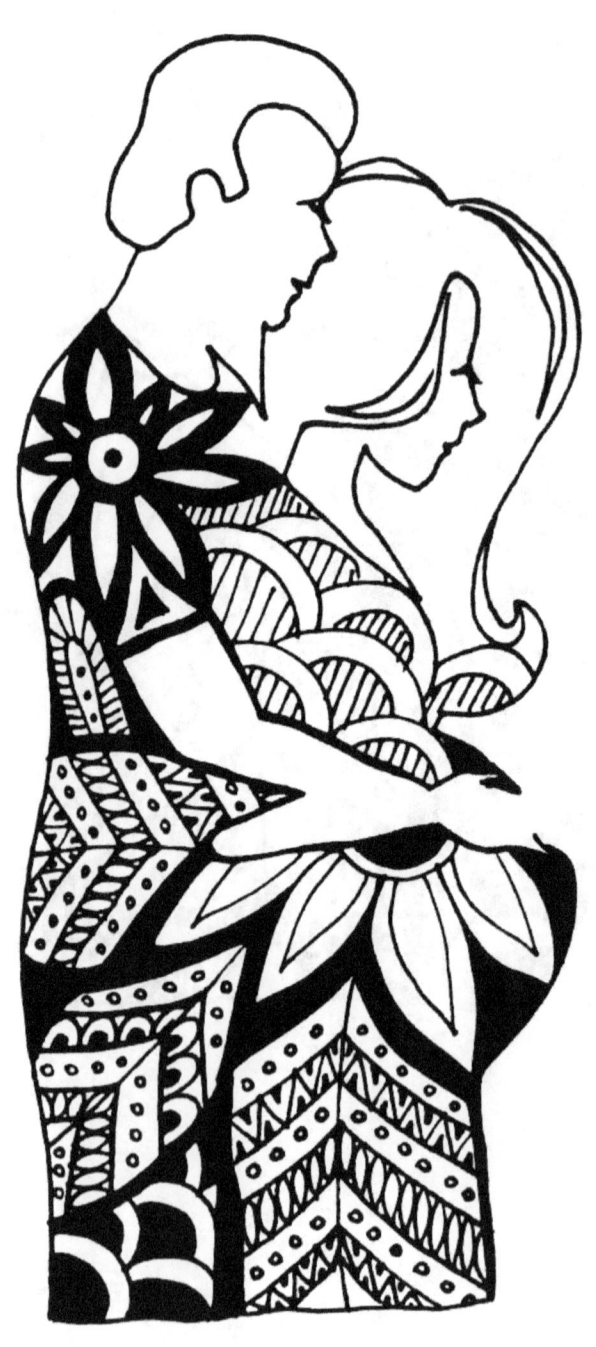

Step 5
Draw some curved parallel lines in different sections in the hairs of the lady.

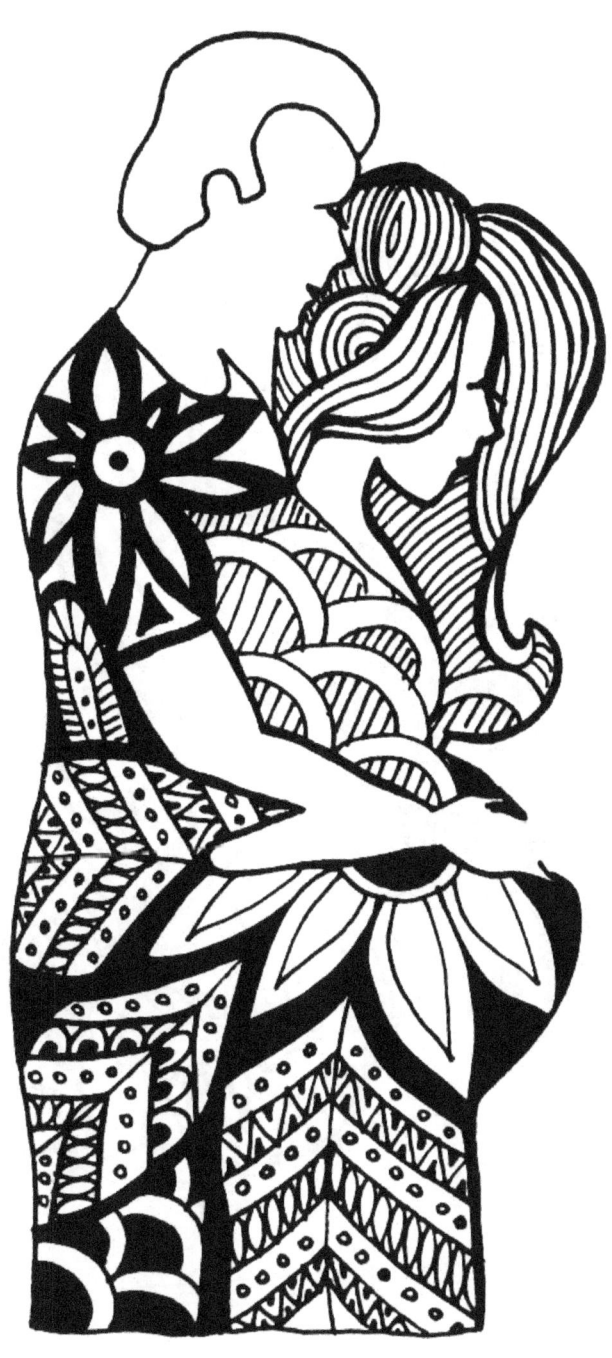

Step 6

Draw some spirals in the hairs of the man. Draw moles like graduating bullets in face, neck and hands of the couple.

The drawing of Zen Doodle pregnant lady in the arms of her husband is complete.

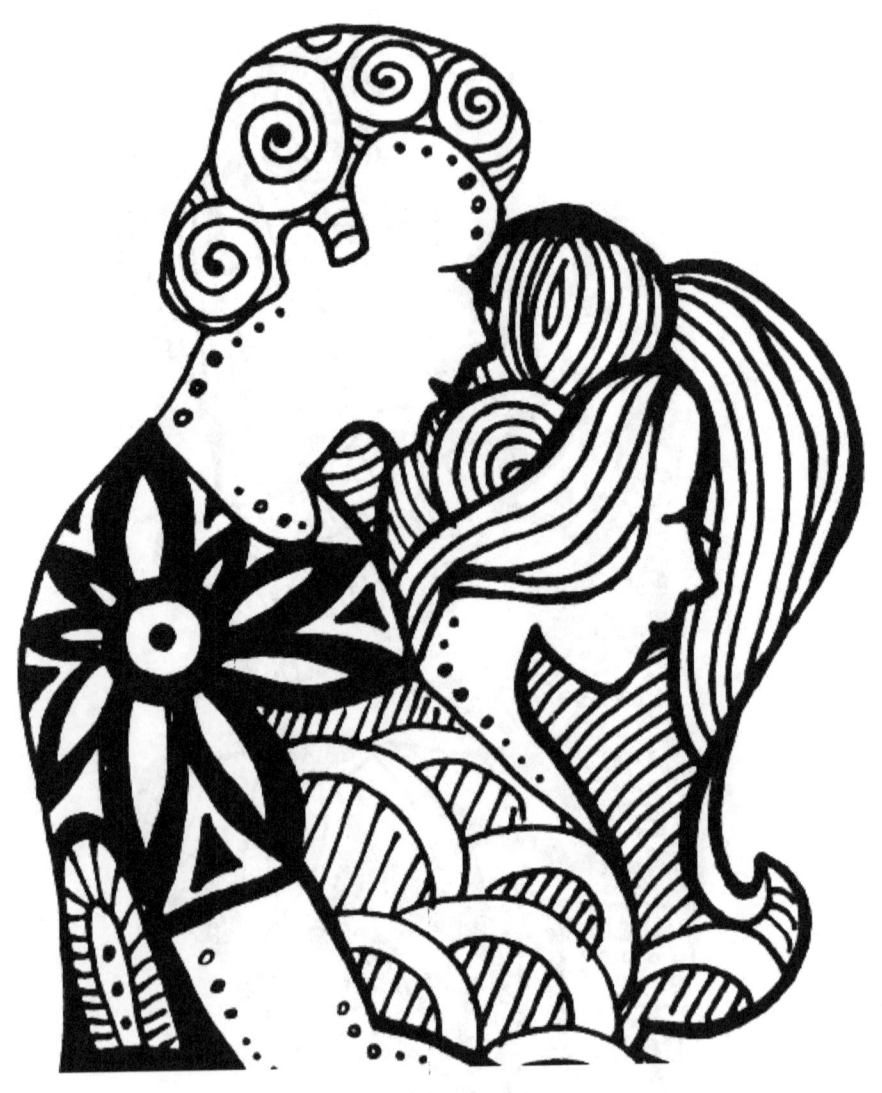

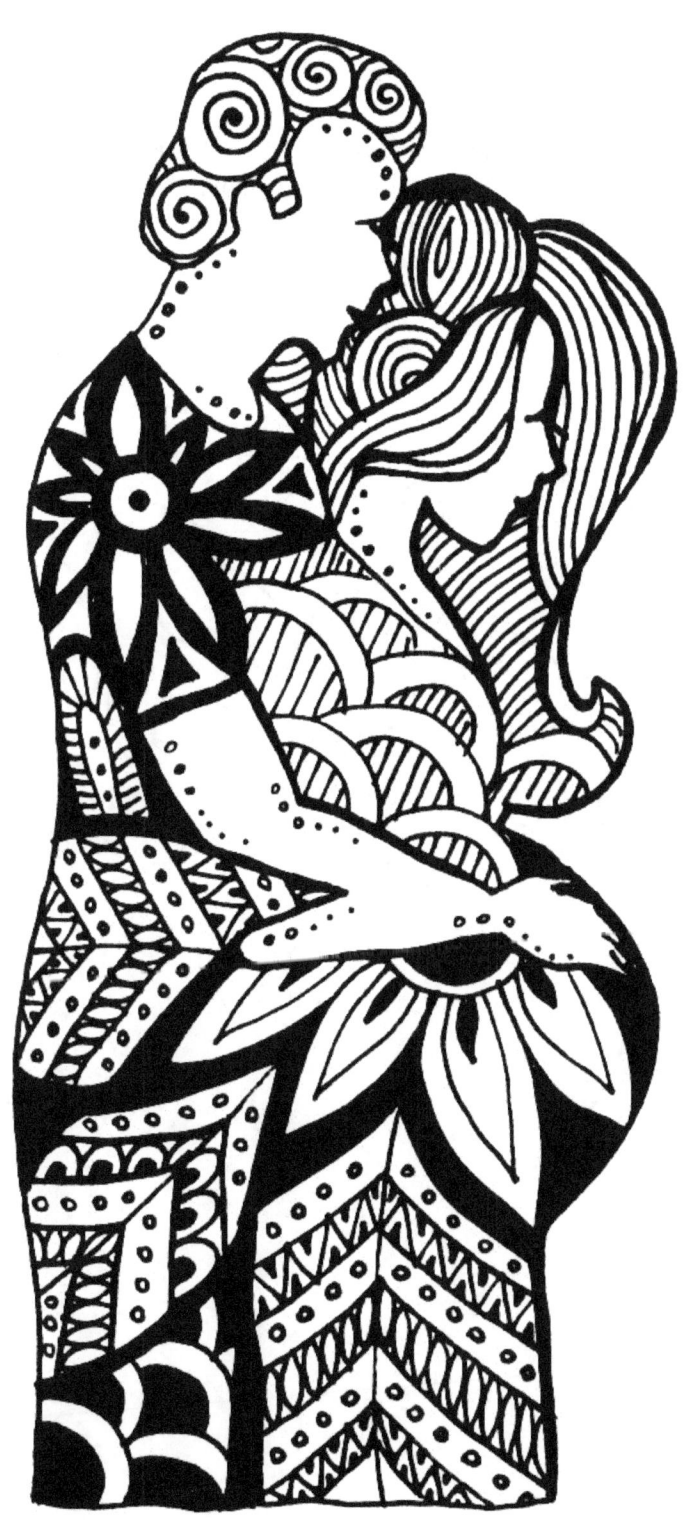

Chapter 6 - The Good Old Fantasies of a Couple

Step 1

Draw the side profile of a couple, seated on either sides of a large heart. You can draw a faint outline of this heart and draw some spirals emerging out of various points in this heart. The lips of the lady are shown in a small pout as if flying a kiss towards the man.

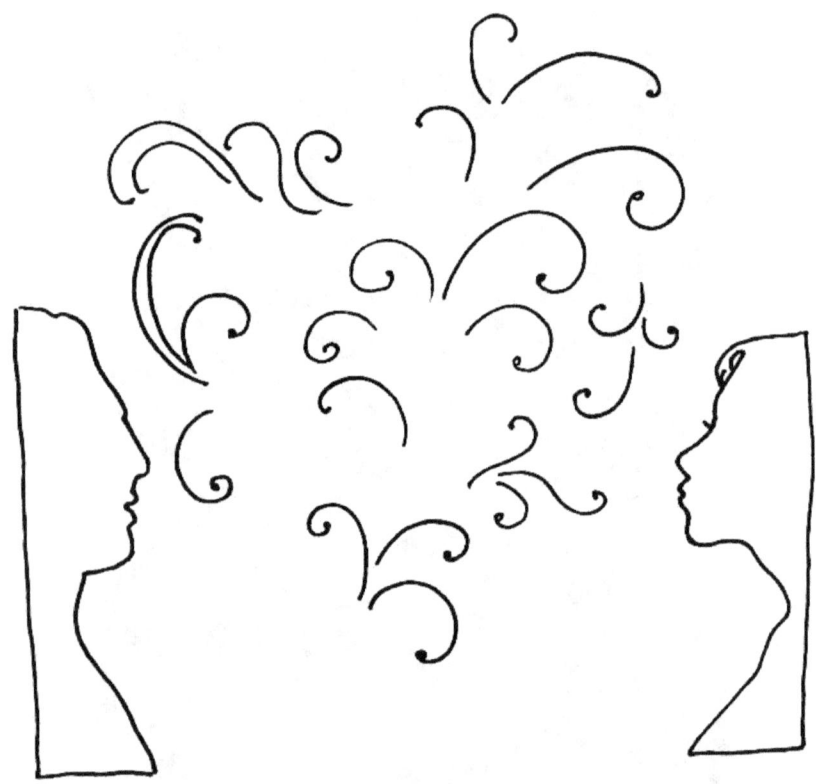

Step 2

Draw some small leaflets emerging out of the spirals like small leaves stem out of a weak branch of a plant.

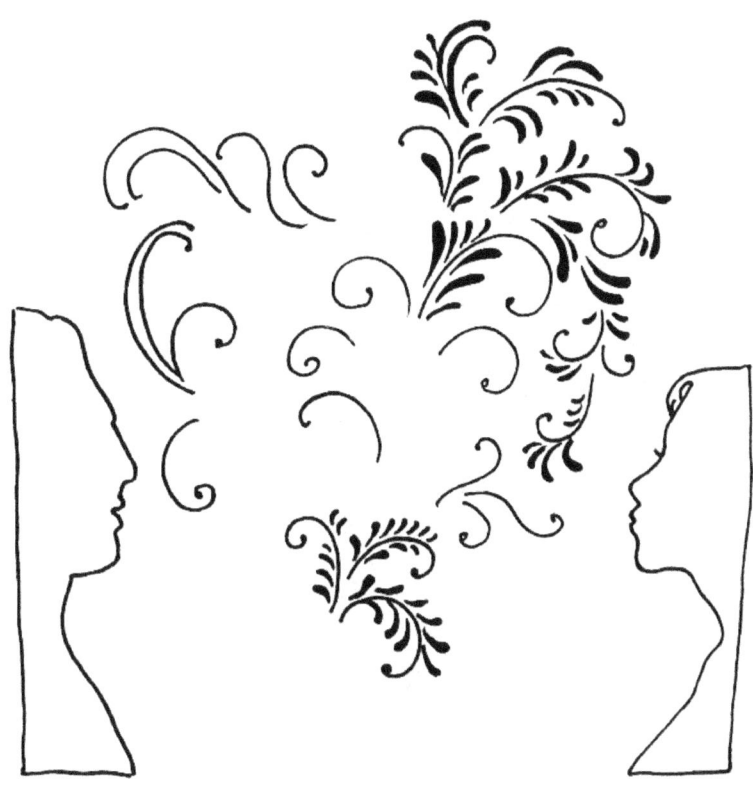

Step 3
Fill the heart completely with these leaflets, spirals, branches and twigs. The outline of the heart is not pronounced yet.

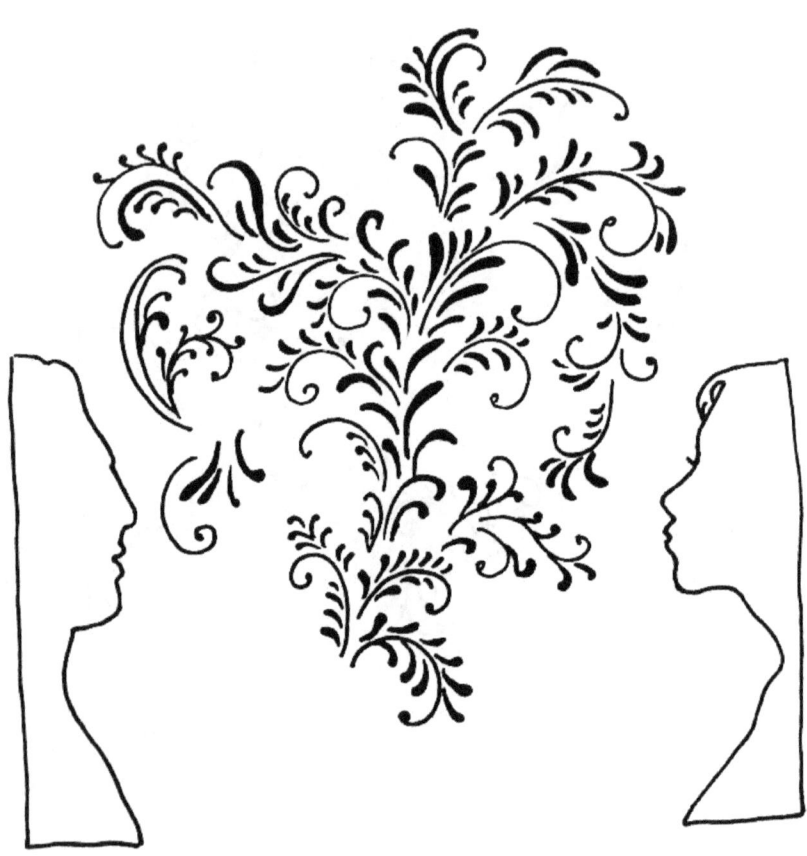

Step 4

Draw a spiral in the chest portion of the man and draw some bullets around the inner side of this spiral. Draw a few elongated leaves stemming out of this spiral and fill them with ink. The leaves should appear solid.

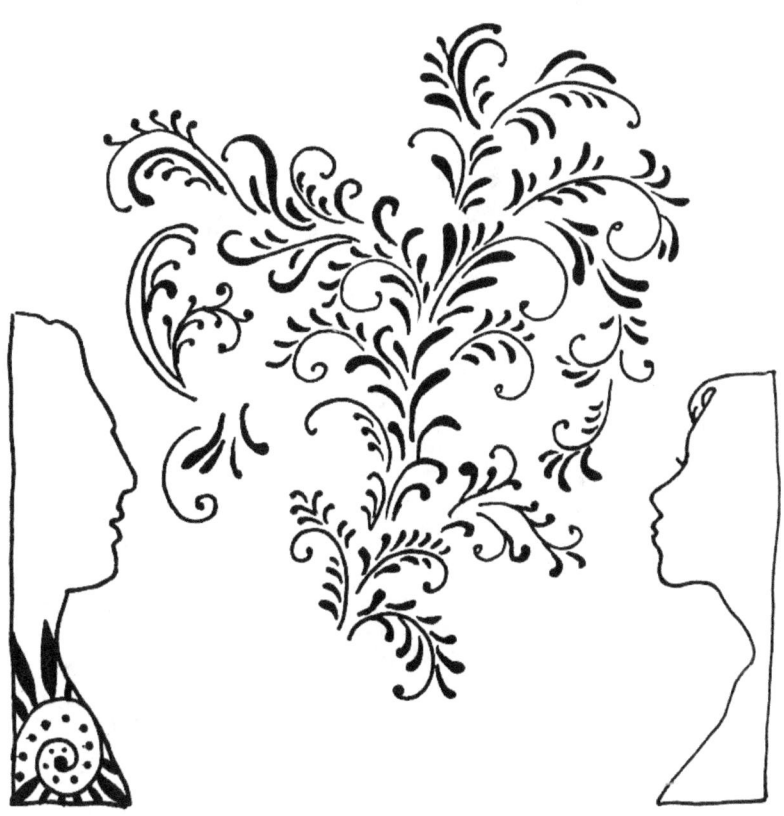

Step 5

Draw a zigzag pattern like a crown on the head of the man. Draw some leaves, smaller in shape, in the topmost portion of the head.

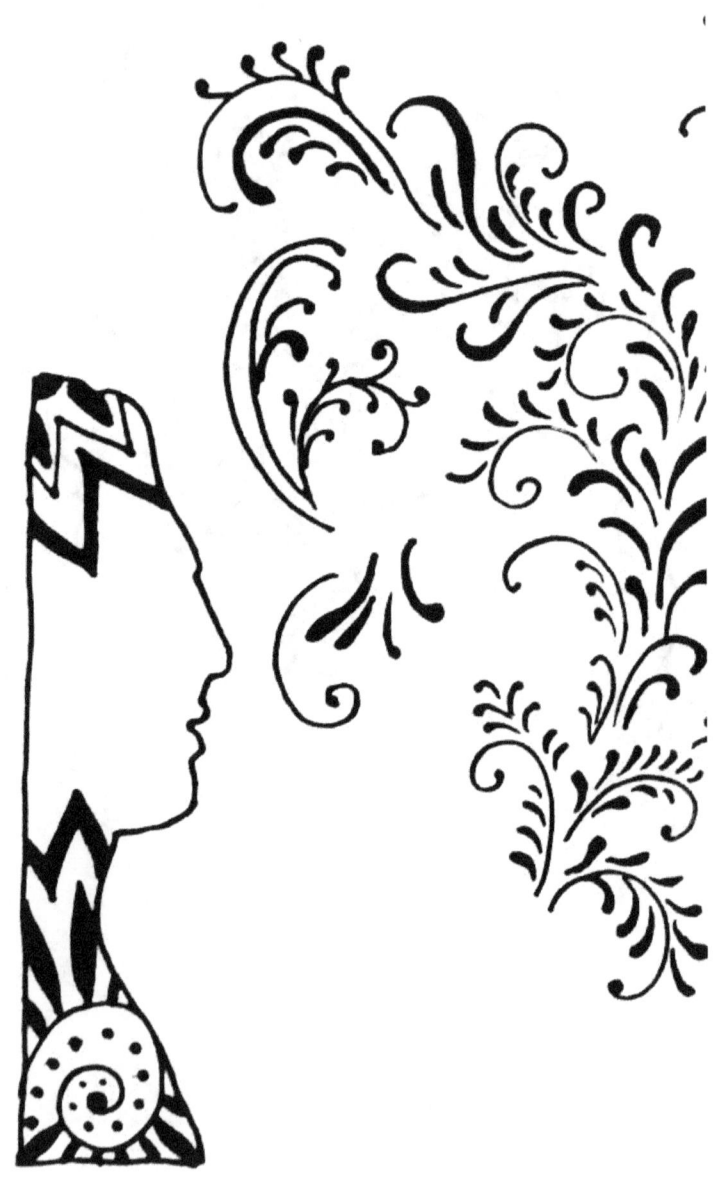

Step 6

Draw some swirls in the face of the man. Draw similar swirls in the face of the woman. In the head of the lady, draw some swirls with parallel outlines. Draw scallops and triangles partially in the neck of the lady and some parallel lines below the neck. In the margins so created, draw some parallel bold lines.

Notice that there is a pencil tip like shape present in the lower left corner of the lady. Draw an arc outside this tip and fill its margins with parallel lines. Draw an outline of the large heart in your drawing, for which you had drawn so many spirals earlier.

Draw two small elongated hearts, one each near the man and the woman, below the large heart. Draw a parallel outline for each of these smaller hearts and fill their margins with different designs as shown in the picture.

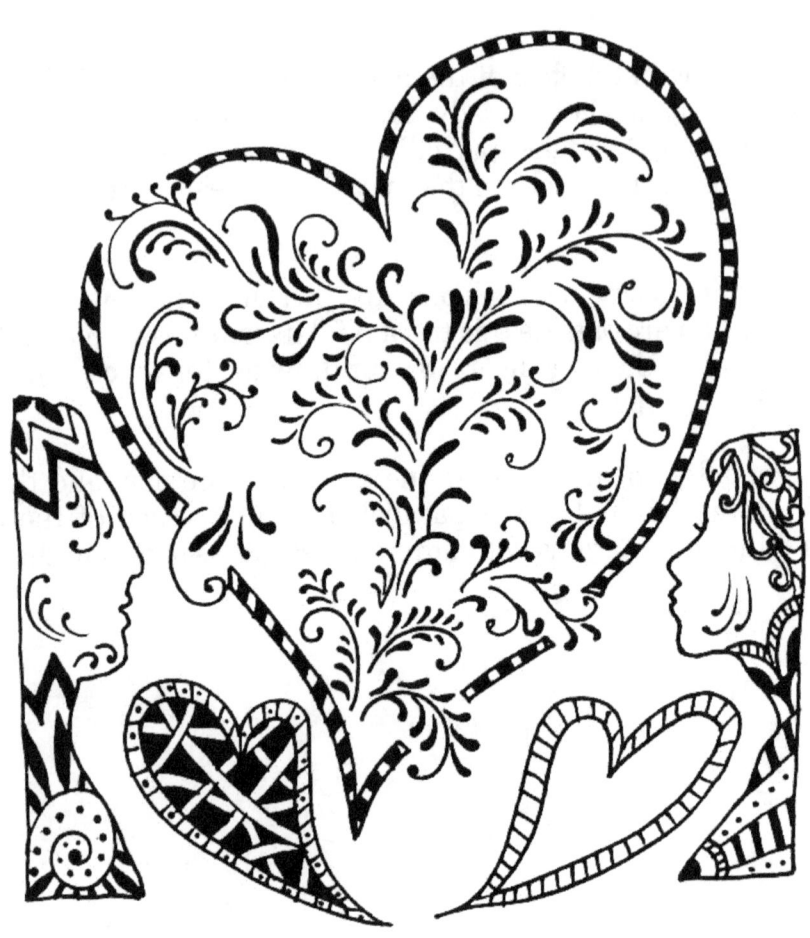

Step 7

In the heart that is closer to the man, draw some shafts with parallel outlines overlapping each other and fill the negative area with ink.

In the heart that is closer to the lady, draw some scallops.

Draw some swirls emerging from the base of these hearts.

The overall drawing should look like a fantasy of a young couple.

Your drawing of the good old fantasies of a couple is complete.

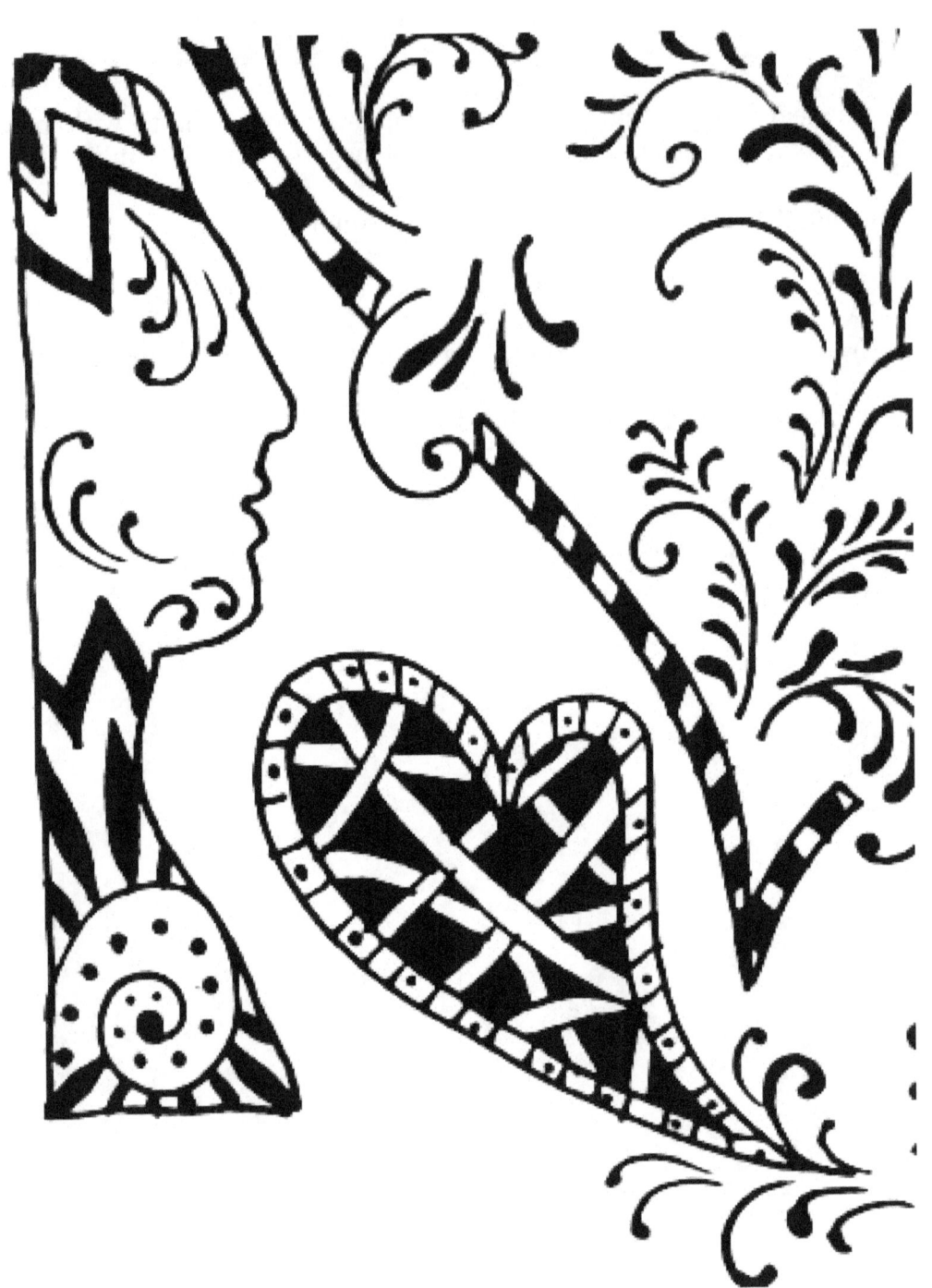

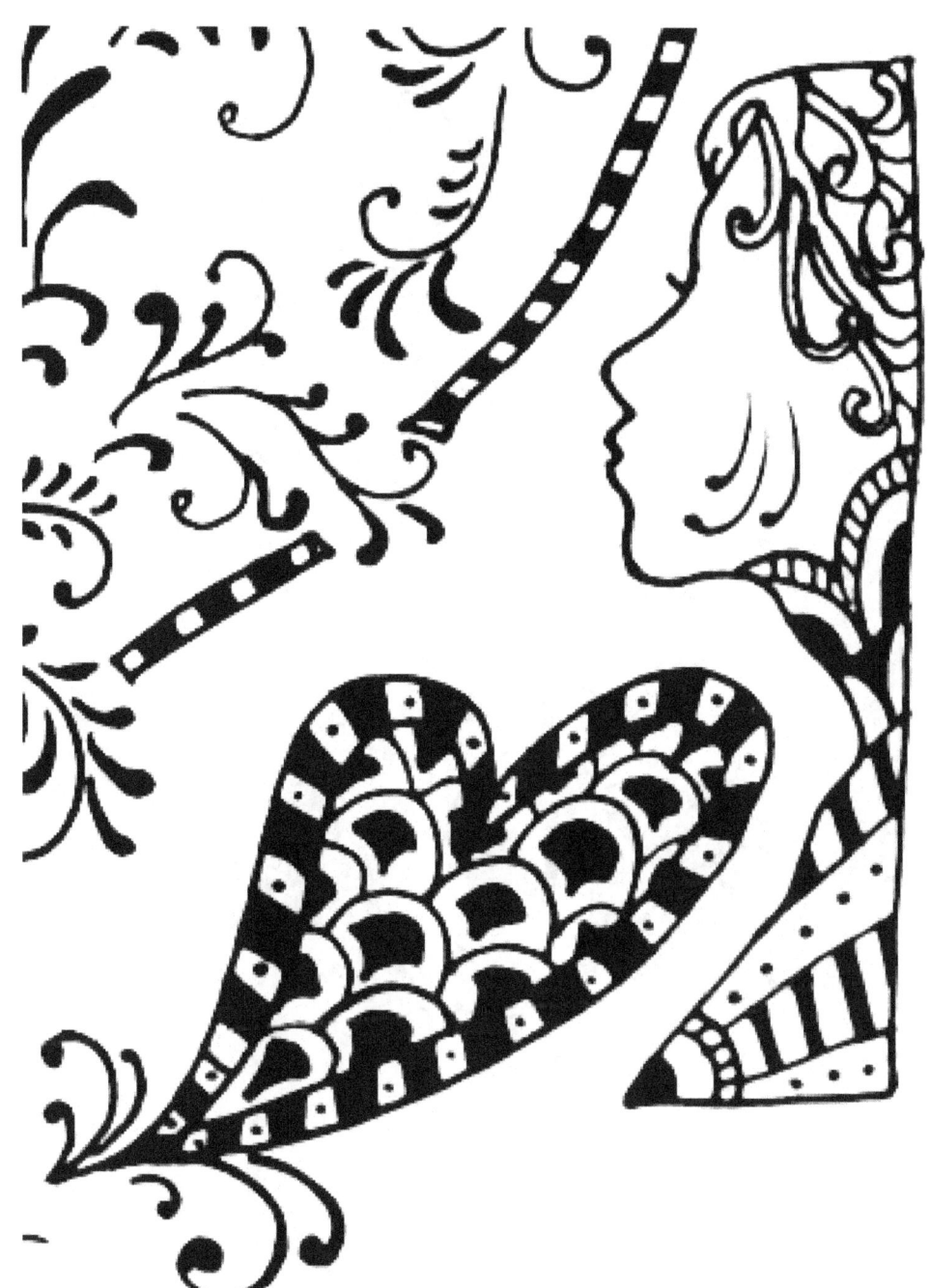

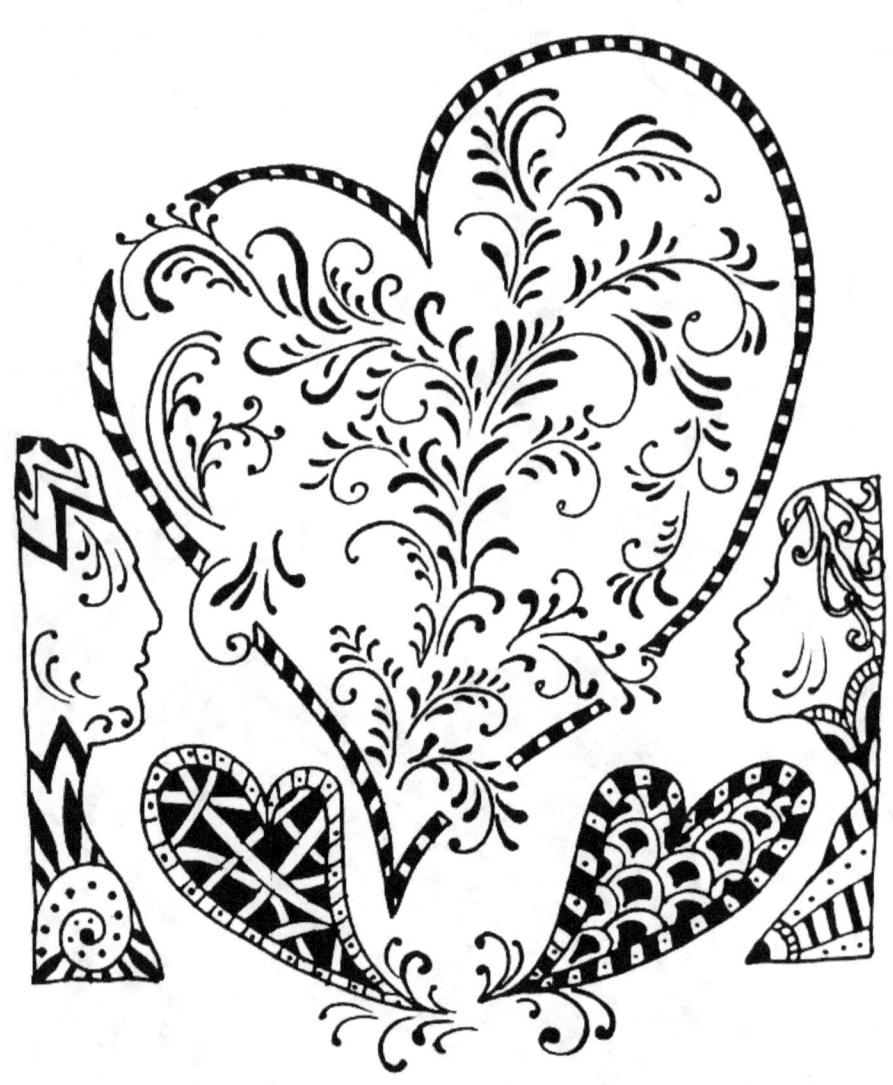

Conclusion

How are you feeling after reading **Drawing People with Zen Doodle Technique?** Good, eh? Did you draw while you were reading? Or you thought that you would draw once you finish the book? Whatsoever, you must not delay anymore and start your practice right now. The genre of Zen Doodle has been in existence for the last many centuries. You can say that as soon as the scripts were invented, man had started learning drawing as well.

You must have read about the drawings of man and animal in the ancient caves of the world. They are nothing but the remains of Zen Doodle. The only difference in the modern drawings of this genre is that we have started refining the drawings and have started thinking strategically about them.

Zen Doodle is not just scribbling on paper. It needs carefully thought figures and filling them up with precisely drawn designs and patterns. Since you have already gone through the drawings of people in this book, you must be feeling confident about drawing them yourself. If you have been shy of drawing people till now, the time has come that you start drawing them now. You can begin with abstract figures and then later jump to realistic figures. However, none of them can be called easy or difficult. Both have their upsides and downsides of drawing.

Drawing Zen Doodle sketches is not much pain. You can practice them even at times when you have nothing productive to do such as waiting for a friend at the metro station, sitting alone in a restraint sipping coffee, etc. You just have to be determined that you want to learn Zen Doodle. Good luck for your learning!

Thank you!

Thank you for choosing our book, we hope you found it interesting and helpful.

If you liked the book, please give us a favor to write your review.

We would really appreciate this!

If you would like to have a bonus – **FREE BOOK**, please send the screenshot of your review to this e-mail: **lucy.artbooks@gmail.com** and we will send you a **FREE BOOK** in PDF as a **GIFT!****

Hope to see you in our future books and good luck in your drawing experience!

** in the e-mail subject please mention the name of the book you reviewed and the author.

Other books from Daniele Ling

ZEN Animals: A Complete Guide to Master Wild Animals Drawing in Zen Doodle

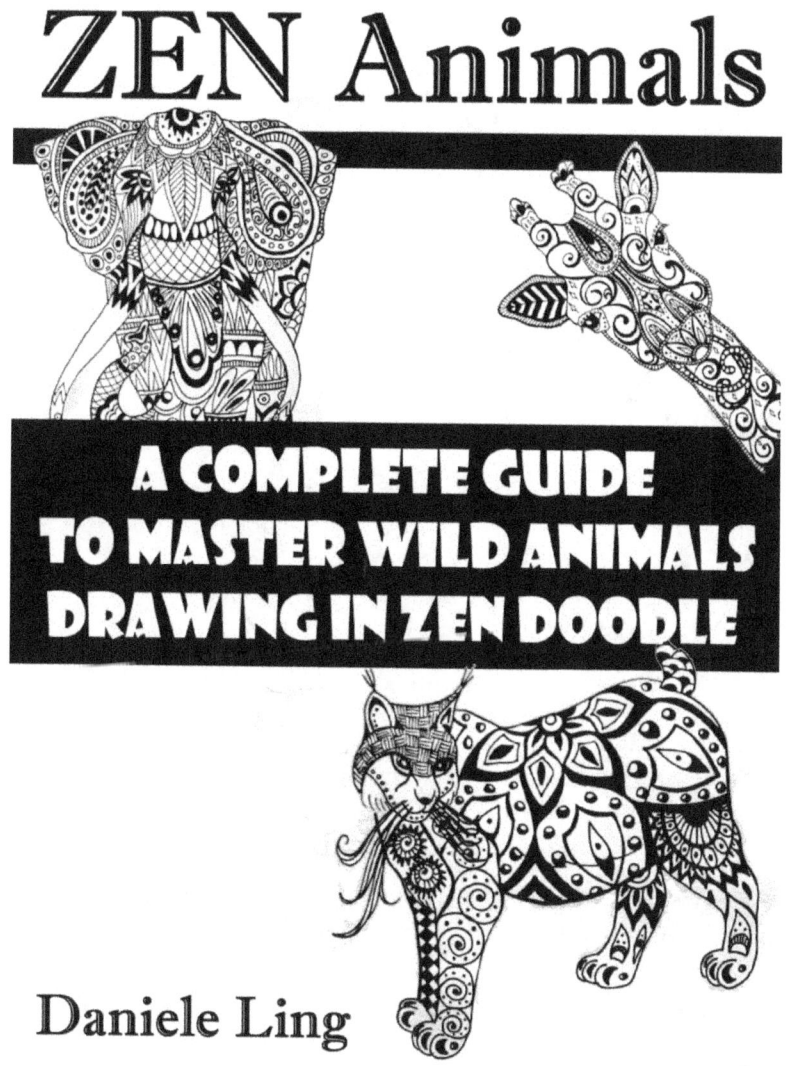

Zen Doodle Cats:
Drawing Zen Doodle Cats Made Easy

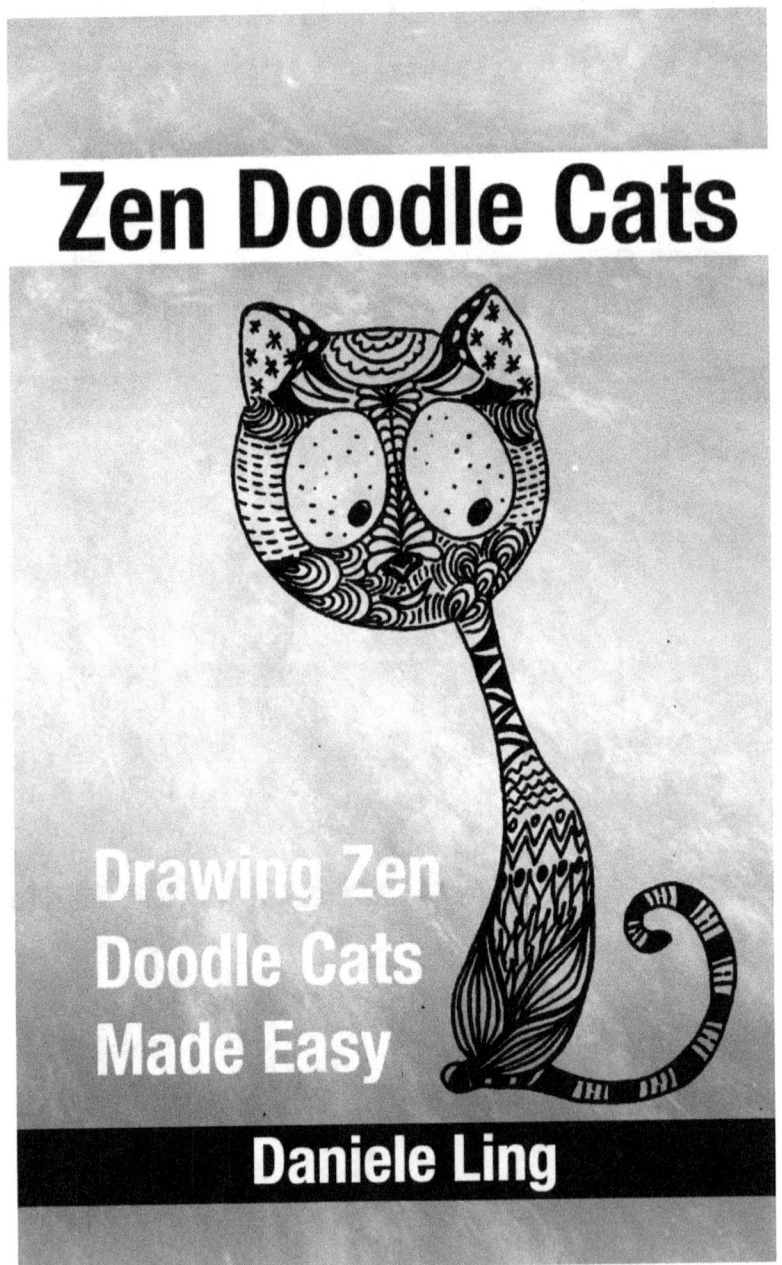

Zen Doodle Imagination:
Create Your Own Zen Doodle Drawings Easy!

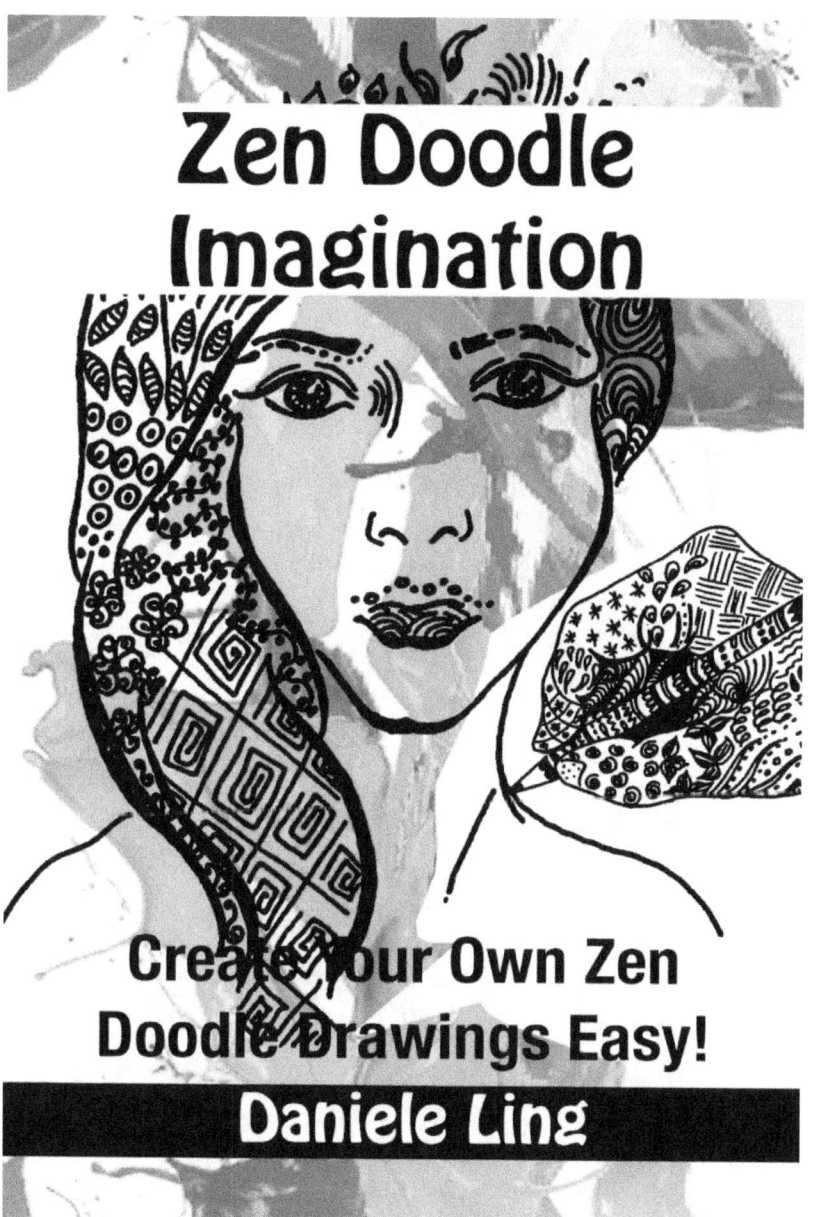

Zen Dogs Drawing:
Learn how to Draw
Your Favorite Dogs with Zen Doodle!

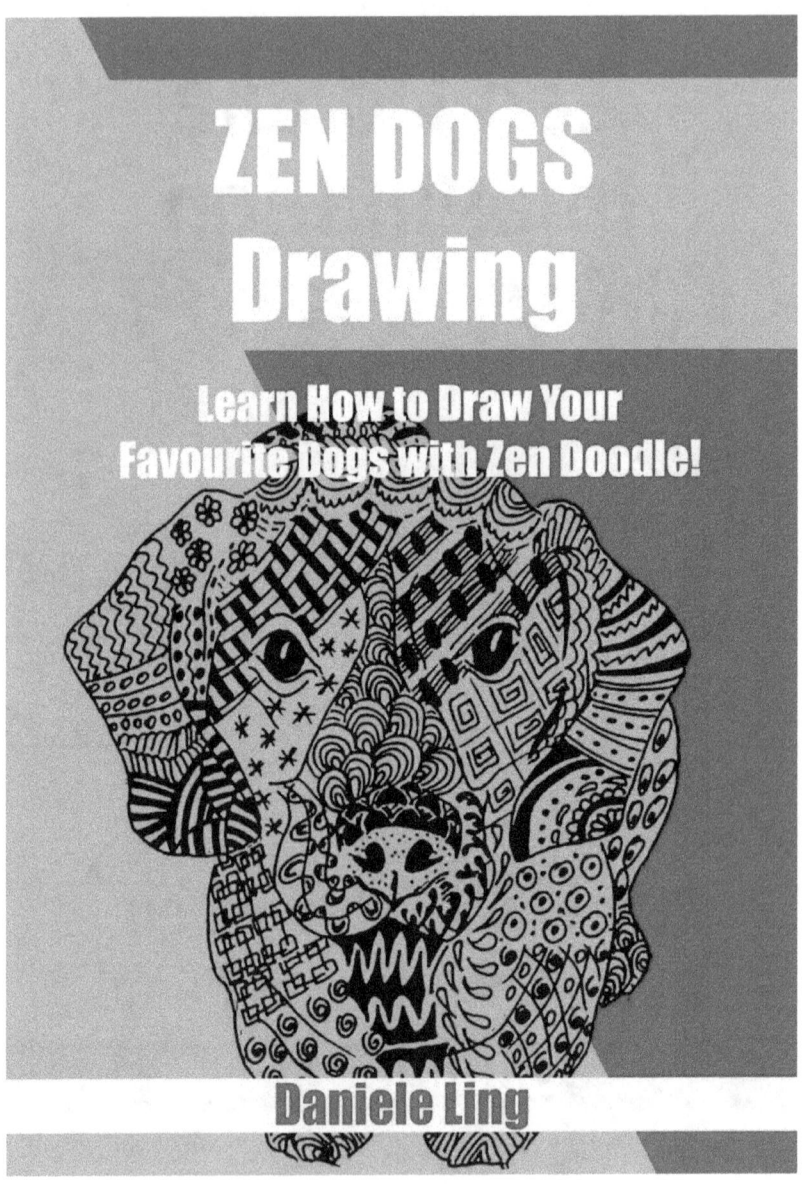

www.ingramcontent.com/pod-product-compliance
Lightning Source LLC
Chambersburg PA
CBHW080722190526
45169CB00006B/2479